Quick and Easy
PANINI PRESS COOKBOOK

Quarto.com

© 2023 Quarto Publishing Group USA Inc.
Text and photography © 2013 Kathy Lipscomb Strahs

First Published in 2023 by New Shoe Press, an imprint of The Quarto Group,
100 Cummings Center, Suite 265-D, Beverly, MA 01915, USA.
T (978) 282-9590 F (978) 283-2742

New Shoe Press titles are also available at discount for retail, wholesale, promotional,
and bulk purchase. For details, contact the Special Sales Manager by email at
specialsales@quarto.com or by mail at The Quarto Group, Attn: Special Sales
Manager, 100 Cummings Center, Suite 265-D, Beverly, MA 01915, USA.

ISBN: 978-0-7603-8372-8
eISBN: 978-0-7603-8373-5

The content in this book was previously published in *The Ultimate Panini Press
Cookbook* (The Harvard Common Press 2013) by Kathy Lipscomb Strahs.

Library of Congress Cataloging-in-Publication Data available

Photography: Kathy Lipscomb Strahs

For Grandma

Quick and Easy
PANINI PRESS
COOKBOOK

Simple Recipes for Delicious Results with any Brand of Panini Makers

KATHY STRAHS

NEW SHOE PRESS

Contents

CHAPTER 1

Panini and Panini Presses

The Basics

Panini Presses—The Ins and Outs

The panini press is, of course, named for the Italian pressed sandwiches that have become so popular here in recent years. You will sometimes see a panini press called simply a "sandwich maker" or an "indoor grill." For the purposes of this book, when I say "panini press" I'm referring to any countertop appliance—including a George Foreman grill— that can heat food between two grates.

That said, as with any appliance, not all panini presses are the same. Some come with a myriad of features and are large enough to accommodate a family's worth of steaks, while others are very basic and designed to fit comfortably in a college dorm room. They're available at all price points, ranging from as little as $20 for a very simple model with a single heat setting to upwards of $300 for one with an LCD screen and removable plates.

People often ask me which type of panini press I recommend. My response is usually "Well, what do you plan to use it for?" I suggest examining five key features to help you determine which panini press meets your needs and your budget:

- Adjustable thermostat
- Grill surface area
- Drainage
- Removable plates
- Adjustable height control

Adjustable Thermostat

An adjustable thermostat allows you to control the amount of heat you're grilling with. Some panini presses allow you to set a specific cooking temperature (350°F, for example); some come with "high," "medium," and "low" settings; some give an adjustable range between "panini" and "sear"; and others are built with a simple on/off switch and no ability to adjust the heat level at all.

If you're planning to grill mainly sandwiches, a panini press without an adjustable thermostat will likely suit your needs. However, the ability to control the temperature is key when grilling certain foods. For my Grilled Rib-Eye Steak (page 73), for instance, I turn the heat up high to get a nice, crusty sear on the meat. To slowly render the fat and crisp the skin on my Grilled Duck Breasts (page 35), I use a medium-low setting. And for my Mini Yellow Layer Cake with Chocolate Buttercream (page 131), which involves baking, I need to set the thermostat exactly to 350°F.

In general, the more heating options, the more expensive the panini press will be. You can buy a press without an adjustable thermostat for as little as $20 or $30; presses with adjustable thermostats typically cost $70 and up.

Grill Surface Area

Some folks prefer a smaller grill due to space constraints in their kitchen or dorm room, or if there are just one or two people in the household. Small grills are also more portable, making them a great option for those who like to bring their panini press on vacation. A large grill surface area is especially beneficial to those who want to make a lot of panini or other foods for a whole family at once—it can be a real timesaver not to have to cook in batches.

Panini presses with large surface areas, accommodating four panini or more, are pricier than small models and usually offer other premium features. They typically range between $70 and $300.

Drainage

If you plan to use your panini press to grill meats, poultry, and other foods beyond panini, it's important to choose a press with drainage features. The grill plates on many panini presses and other indoor grills are designed to drain excess fat, which can make them a healthier cooking alternative. On some models, you

can adjust the plates to tilt forward to allow the fat to flow into a drip pan, while others remain flat and drain via the back of the grill.

Some no-frills panini presses do not have any drainage features at all—you'll notice that the lower plate stays flat and there are no cutouts or sloped edges to allow fat to roll away. Models like these are intended mainly for grilling panini and shouldn't be used for raw meats.

Feature Comparison

You'll find panini presses on the market with features and price points to suit all needs. Here is a rundown of what you can expect to find at the basic, midrange, and premium levels of the panini press spectrum.

Basic ($20–$50)
Pros: Compact size; cooks quickly; affordable
Cons: No adjustable thermostat, drainage feature, removable plates, or adjustable height control; small to medium grill surface area; may not be suitable for grilling raw meats (refer to the manufacturer's instructions)

Midrange ($50–$80)
Pros: May have an adjustable thermostat and drainage feature; larger grill surface area; greater grilling versatility, including raw meats
Cons: Not likely to have removable plates or adjustable height control

Premium ($80–$300)
Pros: Adjustable thermostat; large grill surface area, with drainage feature; may have removable plates; may have adjustable height control; greatest grilling versatility
Cons: Requires more counter space; less portable; less affordable

Removable Plates

Melted and cooked-on bits are a fact of life with the panini press. If your grill has removable plates, cleanup is much easier. You can just pop off the plates and scrub them in the sink or dishwasher. But if your grill doesn't have removable plates, don't despair—I've got helpful cleaning tips for you on page 10.

Adjustable Height Control

I regularly use the adjustable height control feature on my panini press to give me greater flexibility in terms of the types of foods I can grill. This feature allows me to position the upper plate to hover above open-faced sandwiches, make very light contact with soft foods like tomatoes and French toast, and regulate the amount of pressure applied to panini so that the ingredients don't squeeze out. Most panini presses come with a floating hinge, which allows for a degree of pressure control, but very few offer fully adjustable height control.

Whether your panini press comes with all of these features or just one or two, nearly any model will make grilling sandwiches and other foods an easy task.

How to Use a Panini Press

Most panini presses are very easy and straightforward to operate. Here are my tips for getting the best results when it comes to heating, grilling, and cleaning.

Heating

Each panini press model heats differently—some you just plug in, while others have specific heat settings. As you can imagine, this poses quite a challenge for me when it comes to developing recipes that each of you can accurately follow with whichever type of panini press you might have. "High" on one grill might be "sear" on another, and still others have no option to set a heat level at all.

For the vast majority of the recipes in this cookbook, I've suggested setting your panini press to "medium-high" heat. That's a level that's not the highest, but not the lowest—somewhere in between, leaning toward the higher side. (Note: Panini presses with simple on/off heating tend to run on the hotter side, so your cooking time may be shorter with these machines.) The good news is that, for most recipes, the exact temperature won't really matter. Just look at the food you're grilling and decide whether it looks done to you or not. If it's a meat dish, I highly recommend using a meat thermometer (see more discussion on meat thermometers on page 12) to monitor doneness.

Grilling

Notice that I called this section "Grilling." I didn't call it "Flattening" or "Leaning Into the Panini Press to Make Sure the Sandwich Gets Good and Flat." I'm not sure where the practice of pressing down hard on a panini press originated. I see evidence of it over and over again in photos, but it's not what I'd recommend unless you happen to like really flat food. Today's panini presses are designed to provide the right degree of pressure, without any need for you to press down—or flatten—your food.

My recommendation, whether you're making sandwiches or other foods, is that you *grill* them. That is, you place the food on the grates, close the lid so that it's resting on top of the food, and wait until it's done. If you're grilling panini, the sound of melted cheese sizzling on the grates is a good indication that it's time to take the panini off the grill. For meats, I always use a meat thermometer that beeps when the desired temperature has been reached.

Cleaning

As I've mentioned before, if your panini press comes with removable plates, cleanup is relatively easy. Once the grill has cooled down, you just unsnap the grates from the base and wash them in the sink or dishwasher. But what about grills without removable plates? Truth be told, the grill I use most often doesn't have removable plates. No big deal—here's how I get it as clean as new.

Scrape It While It's Hot. More often than not there's melted cheese remaining on the grates after I've grilled panini. It comes with the territory. Thanks to the nonstick coating on the grates, cheese scrapes off easily with the help of the plastic grill scraper that came with my panini press (if yours didn't come with its own grill scraper, see my recommendation for a silicone grill brush on page 13) and a clean cloth. For more stubborn stuck-on food—which often happens when I grill meat, especially with sweet marinades—I unplug the grill and, while it's still hot, I (very carefully) try to loosen and lift off as many bits as possible with the grill scraper. Then I let the grill cool completely. *Safety note:* Make sure the unplugged power cord is resting next to the grill, not dangling where it could accidentally be pulled and drag the panini press off the table or counter. And never use an abrasive pad on the grill as it may damage the nonstick coating.

Take It to the Sink. Once the grill has cooled, I bring it over to the counter adjacent to the kitchen sink (let me reiterate—the grill *must be unplugged* before you bring it anywhere near water). I position the grill so that the front edge is just above the bowl of the sink. Then I squirt on some dish soap and wash the lower plate with a wet sponge and use a silicone grill brush to get to those hidden places between the grates. Once it's clean, I use the pull-out faucet to rinse off the plate and then dry it with paper towels (just in case I missed any bits of blackened cooked-on food that would stain my nice kitchen towels). If your sink doesn't have a pull-out faucet, you can also rinse with a very wet sponge. *Safety note:* As with all electrical appliances, don't ever let the electrical connection get wet and *never* submerge any part of the panini press itself in water.

Turn It Upside Down. And what about that upper plate, you ask? Cleaning that had been a challenge for me until I discovered an easy solution—I turn the entire machine on its end so that the upper plate lies flat on the counter over the sink. Then I can clean it just as I did with the lower plate. Just be aware that with this new distribution of weight—the upper plate is typically much lighter than the lower plate—the press may be less stable, so work carefully.

Remember the Drip Tray. Some panini presses come equipped with a drip tray that is so well concealed that it's easy to forget about it. Especially after grilling meats and vegetables, it's important to clean out any fat or juices that may have accumulated.

Grilling Beyond Sandwiches

Anyone who believes that a panini press is useful only for grilling sandwiches is missing out on a whole world of possibilities. We're talking about a tool with two direct heating sources—which, by the way, heat up in under five minutes. There's really no limit to what it can grill—unless, of course, the manufacturer of your grill suggests limits. Always abide by your product's manual.

Meat, Poultry, and Seafood

Grilling meat, poultry, and seafood on the panini press is not only a healthy way to cook but also, with the ability to grill both sides of your food at once, a much faster technique than outdoor grilling or oven roasting. Especially in the summertime, when it's often too hot to turn on the stove or stand over a hot outdoor grill, the panini press can become your best friend when it comes to getting dinner on the table. Be sure to have a drip tray in place to collect any grease that runs off (and be sure to keep this book away from the grill to avoid the side spatter!). If your press does not come equipped with a drain and/or drip tray, I don't recommend using it for grilling raw meats.

So how long will it take to cook your meat and poultry on the panini press? I'll say it again: a meat thermometer will take all the guesswork out of determining when the food is done (see page 12). Just insert the thermometer and wait until the desired temperature is reached. The United States Department of Agriculture (USDA) recommends the following safe internal cooking temperatures:

Food	Temperature
Beef, pork, lamb, and veal steaks, chops, and roasts	145°F
Ground beef, pork, lamb, and veal	160°F
Poultry	165°F

You'll find a slew of recipes for grilled meats in this cookbook—everything from rib-eye steak (page 73) and bratwurst (page 52) to brined turkey thigh (page 31) and seared ahi (page 88).

Fruits and Vegetables

Whether I'm grilling zucchini or eggplant, bananas or peaches, it's all made easy with the panini press. I'll usually toss vegetables in a little olive oil, season with salt and pepper, and grill till they're tender. With fruit, often just a brush of melted butter is all that's needed to get those beautiful dark grill marks and a lightly crisp crust on the outside.

A real advantage to grilling fruits and vegetables on the panini press, as opposed to an outdoor grill, is the food won't fall through the grates. This means you can grill green beans, asparagus, and any other long, skinny, or tiny produce item you can think of, and everything will stay in place on the grill.

Baking

Yes, baking. It's not the first task most people attempt with their panini press (or even the second or the third), but it's possible to do it. My secret weapon for baking on a panini press is a ramekin, a small straight-sided ceramic dish. I just fill a ramekin with my cake batter, frittata mixture, or anything else I might normally bake in the oven, close the grill lid, and wait till it's done. I've used this method to make a variety of individual-sized dishes such as quinoa cakes (page 106).

Tools of the Trade

In addition to a good panini press, the following tools will make preparing and grilling panini even easier.

Cheese Slicer. As I've mentioned, slicing your own cheese is often the best way to go from a melting and ease-of-layering standpoint. A basic cheese plane or slicer isn't expensive, typically $10 to $1You want one that is comfortable to grip, and with a metal blade that can stand up to slicing firmer cheeses without bending itself out of shape. I use the Calphalon dual-edge cheese plane.

Cheese Grater. Yes, slicing your own cheese is usually best, but I do grate some cheeses, especially Parmesan and other harder cheeses that take longer to melt. You can also use the grater for zesting lemons and limes as well as for finely grating garlic and onions. I prefer a box grater for these jobs. They're available at all price points, but I have to say that I have had a much easier time grating since I upgraded to a higher-end Microplane model.

Serrated Knife. A sturdy serrated knife will allow you to slice through your panini cleanly without placing undue pressure on your ingredients. Even better—although it's a bit of a splurge—is an offset knife, which you'll often see used in panini cafés and restaurants. The offset design allows you to bring the knife all the way down to the cutting board without your knuckles getting in the way.

Meat Thermometer. If you're going to grill meats on your panini press, I highly recommend using a meat thermometer. It's the easiest and most reliable way to ensure that meat is cooked to the desired temperature. With the OXO model I have, it's easy for me to set the temperature (it comes with preset USDA and chef recommendations), insert the probe into the meat I'm grilling, place the meat on the panini press, close the lid, and wait until the thermometer beeps to tell me that the meat is done. It eliminates all of the guesswork, and I don't lose any heat by having to open the lid repeatedly to check for doneness.

Silicone Spatula and Tongs. Everything you place on the grill has to come off at some point. For this task, you'll want a silicone spatula and silicone tongs. They easily lift your food without causing any damage to the nonstick surface of the panini press.

Silicone Grill Brush. Many grills come equipped with their own grill scraper, but for those that don't, you will probably find a silicone grill brush very helpful when it comes time to clean your panini press. The soft-yet-firm bristles make it easy to scrape up the cooked-on bits that can get trapped between the grates without damaging the nonstick coating. OXO makes the excellent grill brush that I use.

Silicone Basting Brush. For brushing olive oil onto bread, vegetables, black bean patties, and more, a silicone basting or pastry brush is a useful tool. It distributes oil evenly and goes right into the dishwasher for cleanup.

CHAPTER 2

Poultry Perfection

Chicken, Turkey, and Duck on the Panini Press

Chicken Cordon Bleu Panini

It's time to take things a little retro. Chicken cordon bleu (which translates to "blue ribbon") may not have actually originated at the famed French cooking school, but it was nonetheless a winning dish for many American families in the 1960s and '70s. The key components—breaded chicken breast, cheese, and ham—transform easily into a sandwich, along with a sweet kick of honey mustard.

CHICKEN

2 boneless, skinless chicken breasts, halved horizontally to create 4 cutlets (about 1 pound total)

½ teaspoon coarse salt

⅛ teaspoon freshly ground black pepper

½ cup all-purpose flour

1 large egg, beaten

½ cup plain bread crumbs

2 tablespoons extra-virgin olive oil

PANINI

¼ cup honey

¼ cup Dijon mustard

4 tablespoons (½ stick) butter, at room temperature

8 slices rustic white bread, sliced from a dense bakery loaf

4 ounces sliced ham

4 ounces Swiss cheese, sliced

—

4 panini

CHICKEN: Season the chicken with salt and pepper on both sides. Set up a dredging station with the flour, beaten egg, and bread crumbs each in its own separate shallow bowl. In a large skillet, heat the olive oil over medium-high heat. Dredge each piece of chicken in the flour, then the egg, then the bread crumbs, and place it carefully in the skillet. Cook the chicken for 3 to 4 minutes on each side. Transfer the chicken to a wire rack or a paper towel–lined plate to drain.

PANINI: Heat the panini press to medium-high heat.

Whisk together the honey and Dijon mustard in a small bowl.

FOR EACH SANDWICH: Spread butter on two slices of bread to flavor the outside of the sandwich. Flip over both slices and spread 1 tablespoon honey mustard on the other side of each slice. Top one slice with a breaded chicken breast, followed by ham and cheese slices. Close the sandwich with the other slice of bread, buttered side up.

Grill two panini at a time, with the lid closed, until the cheese is melted and the bread is toasted, 4 to 5 minutes.

Garlic Chicken Panini

Rest assured, the garlic flavor in these panini comes from the basil-garlic mayonnaise, and it isn't overwhelming. You can still kiss your loved ones after eating these sandwiches . . . which is a good thing, because someone will definitely want to kiss you if you make one for them.

CHICKEN

4 cups water

¼ cup coarse salt

2 tablespoons honey

1 bay leaf

1 garlic clove, crushed

6 whole black peppercorns

A pinch of dried thyme

A pinch of dried parsley

1 tablespoon freshly squeezed lemon juice

2 boneless, skinless chicken breasts, halved horizontally to create 4 cutlets (about 1 pound total)

PANINI

1 French baguette, cut into 4 portions, or 4 mini baguettes

1 recipe Basil-Garlic Mayonnaise (recipe follows)

½ cup sliced marinated artichoke hearts

½ cup sliced roasted red bell peppers

4 ounces Swiss cheese, sliced

—

4 panini

CHICKEN: In a large bowl, combine the water, salt, honey, bay leaf, garlic, peppercorns, thyme, parsley, and lemon juice until the salt and honey are dissolved. Add the chicken, cover the bowl with plastic wrap, and let soak in the brine for 30 to 40 minutes in the refrigerator.

PANINI: Heat the panini press to medium-high heat. If your panini press comes with a removable drip tray, make sure it is in place (see page 11).

Remove the chicken from the brine and discard the brine. Pat the chicken cutlets dry and transfer them to the grill. Close the lid and grill the chicken until it's cooked to an internal temperature of 165°F, 3 to 4 minutes. Set the chicken aside. Unplug the grill, carefully wipe it clean, and heat it again to medium-high heat.

FOR EACH SANDWICH: Slice off the domed top of a baguette portion to create a flat grilling surface. Split the baguette to create top and bottom halves. Spread 1 tablespoon of basil-garlic mayonnaise inside each baguette half. Place a chicken cutlet on the bottom baguette half and top it with artichoke hearts, roasted red bell peppers, and cheese. Close the sandwich.

Grill two panini at a time, with the lid closed, until the cheese is melted and the baguettes are toasted, 5 to 7 minutes.

Basil-Garlic Mayonnaise

½ cup coarsely chopped fresh basil

1 garlic clove, smashed

⅛ teaspoon coarse salt

A dash of cayenne pepper

½ cup mayonnaise

—

About ½ cup

Blend the basil, garlic, salt, and cayenne in a food processor until well combined. Add the mayonnaise and continue to blend until smooth. Transfer the mayonnaise to a small bowl, cover, and refrigerate for 30 minutes to allow the flavors to meld.

Pulled BBQ Chicken Panini

Napkins were made so that we could partake of sandwiches like this. We're talking about shredded rotisserie chicken simmered in barbecue sauce, piled on Italian bread, drizzled with chili oil, and topped with fresh mozzarella and caramelized onions. That's worth a little untidiness, right? Look for chili oil, a spicy condiment that's been infused with chili peppers, alongside other oils or in the Asian foods section of your grocery store.

2½ cups barbecue sauce

1 whole rotisserie chicken, skin and bones removed, meat shredded

6 Italian rolls, such as *filone* or ciabatta

1 cup Caramelized Onions (recipe follows)

12 ounces fresh mozzarella cheese, thinly sliced

Chili oil for brushing (optional)

—

6 panini

In a medium-size saucepan, bring the barbecue sauce to a simmer over medium heat. Add the shredded chicken and continue to simmer for another 10 minutes.

Heat the panini press to medium-high heat.

For each sandwich: Split a roll to create top and bottom halves. Scoop a generous amount of pulled BBQ chicken on the bottom half of the roll, followed by some caramelized onions and several slices of mozzarella. Close the sandwich with the top half of the roll and brush a little chili oil on the surface, if desired.

Grill three panini at a time, with the lid closed, until the cheese is melted and the rolls are toasted, 4 to 5 minutes.

Caramelized Onions

It is well worth the time it takes to allow these silky onion ribbons to slowly cook down to their deep brown caramelized state. You can use the onions right away or store them in a covered container in the refrigerator for up to a week. Consider making a double batch so you'll have plenty on hand.

1 tablespoon extra-virgin olive oil

3 medium-size onions (white, yellow, or red), halved and thinly sliced

Coarse salt and freshly ground black pepper

—

About 1 cup

Heat the olive oil in a large skillet over medium heat. Add the onions and cook for 10 minutes, stirring occasionally. The onions will be soft and just barely beginning to turn brown.

Reduce the heat to low. Season with salt and pepper and continue to cook, stirring often to prevent scorching, until the onions are soft, deep brown, and caramelized, another 40 to 50 minutes.

Lemon-Thyme Chicken Panini

If you love bright, tangy Mediterranean flavors, these panini are for you. The chicken breasts are infused with lemon zest and thyme in a quick brine, then grilled in just a few minutes on the panini press. Then they're made into panini with feta–goat cheese spread, sweet sun-dried tomatoes, and arugula. These are great panini to pack in an insulated bag to take to work or on a picnic.

CHICKEN

4 cups water

¼ cup coarse salt

2 tablespoons honey

1 bay leaf

6 whole black peppercorns

1 teaspoon dried thyme

2 teaspoons grated lemon zest

1 tablespoon freshly squeezed lemon juice

2 boneless, skinless chicken breasts, halved horizontally to create 4 cutlets (about 1 pound total)

PANINI

4 tablespoons (½ stick) butter, at room temperature

8 slices rustic white bread, sliced from a dense bakery loaf

1 recipe Feta–Goat Cheese Spread (recipe follows)

1 cup baby arugula

½ cup sliced oil-packed sun-dried tomatoes

—

4 panini

CHICKEN: In a large bowl, stir together the water, salt, honey, bay leaf, peppercorns, thyme, lemon zest, and lemon juice until the salt and honey are dissolved. Add the chicken, cover the bowl with plastic wrap, and let the chicken soak in the brine for 30 to 40 minutes in the refrigerator.

PANINI: Heat the panini press to medium-high heat. If your panini press comes with a removable drip tray, make sure it is in place (see page 11).

Remove the chicken from the brine and discard the brine. Pat the chicken cutlets dry and place them on the grill. Close the lid and grill the chicken until it's cooked to an internal temperature of 165°F, 3 to 4 minutes.

FOR EACH SANDWICH: Spread butter on two slices of bread to flavor the outside of the sandwich. Flip over both slices of bread and spread a generous layer of feta–goat cheese spread on the other side of each. Top one slice with a grilled chicken cutlet, followed by a layer of arugula and sun-dried tomatoes. Close the sandwich with the other slice of bread, buttered side up.

Grill two panini at a time, with the lid closed, until the sandwich is heated through and the bread is toasted, 2 to 3 minutes.

Feta-Goat Cheese Spread

This tangy, soft cheese spread reminds me of the ones my mom would sometimes treat my sisters and me to after school. We'd feel very grown up as we assembled simple little canapés for ourselves on crackers. Tasty spreads like this also make quick panini ingredients, with no melting necessary.

1 (5½-ounce) log goat cheese, at room temperature

1 ounce (about ¼ cup) crumbled feta cheese

1 tablespoon heavy cream or half-and-half

⅛ teaspoon freshly ground black pepper

—

About ½ cup

In a mini food processor or in a medium-size bowl with a hand mixer, beat together the goat cheese, feta, cream, and black pepper until whipped and fluffy.

Turkey and Wild Mushroom Panini

My husband was away at a conference in Las Vegas when I emailed him about these panini. I couldn't wait to tell him that I'd come up with a turkey and mushroom sandwich that I loved.

1 ciabatta loaf, cut into 4 portions, or 4 ciabatta rolls

1 recipe Sautéed Wild Mushrooms (recipe follows)

4 ounces watercress

8 ounces carved or deli-sliced roast turkey

4 ounces Swiss cheese, sliced

3 tablespoons Dijon mustard

—
4 panini

Heat the panini press to medium-high heat.

FOR EACH SANDWICH: Split a ciabatta portion to create top and bottom halves. Spoon a generous layer of mushrooms inside the bottom half, followed by a handful of watercress and a few slices of turkey and cheese. Spread Dijon mustard inside the top half and place it on top.

Grill two panini at a time, with the lid closed, until the cheese is melted and the ciabatta is toasted, 4 to 5 minutes.

Sautéed Wild Mushrooms

There aren't many foods that can't be remarkably enhanced by sautéing them in butter with garlic and shallots and finishing them with some balsamic vinegar.

1 tablespoon extra-virgin olive oil

1 tablespoon unsalted butter

¼ cup thinly sliced shallots

2 garlic cloves, minced

2½ cups sliced wild mushrooms, such as shiitake (stemmed), chanterelle, or porcini

2 teaspoons balsamic vinegar

1 tablespoon chopped fresh parsley

Coarse salt and freshly ground black pepper

—
About 1¼ cups

Heat the olive oil and butter in a large skillet over medium heat until the butter is melted. Add the shallots and garlic and cook, stirring frequently, until they're fragrant, 1 to 2 minutes. Add the mushrooms and cook, stirring occasionally, until the mushrooms are tender, 5 to 7 minutes. Stir in the balsamic vinegar and parsley and season with salt and pepper to taste.

No-Fuss, No-Flip Chicken Quesadillas

I'll tell you one thing that really impresses me: when chefs can easily and expertly flip food in a skillet with just a quick flick of the wrist. I watch in complete awe—this is not a skill I currently possess. I can usually flip pancakes if the batter is thick enough, but a quesadilla full of shredded cheese and other loose toppings? Forget it.

Enter the panini press, with its ability to cook from both the top and bottom at the same time. It's by far the easiest way that I know of to cook quesadillas and other dishes that you'd otherwise have to flip.

1 tablespoon vegetable oil

8 (8-inch) flour tortillas

8 ounces (about 2 cups) shredded cheese, such as cheddar, Monterey Jack, or Colby, or a mixture

1 (4-ounce) can diced green chiles, drained

1 cup shredded cooked chicken

Salsa, for serving

—

4 quesadillas

Heat the panini press to medium-high heat.

FOR EACH QUESADILLA: Brush a little oil on two tortillas. Flip over one tortilla and scatter on a few tablespoons of cheese, leaving a 1-inch margin around the edge to avoid too much ooze during melting. Top the cheese with a few tablespoons of green chiles, some shredded chicken, and more cheese. Place the other tortilla, oiled side up, on top.

Carefully transfer one quesadilla to the grill and close the lid. Grill the quesadilla until the cheese is melted and the tortilla is crisped, 3 to 4 minutes. Repeat with the rest of the tortillas.

Cut the quesadillas into wedges and serve with salsa.

Chicken Teriyaki

I knew from the outset that chicken teriyaki would be well suited for a minimal effort–high reward meal on the panini press. Boneless chicken cooks incredibly quickly on the grill, and you can set it in its sweet and salty marinade ahead of time. All I needed was to research the right ingredients to make an authentically Japanese version of this familiar favorite. I found such an approach on Marc Matsumoto's popular food blog, NoRecipes.com. Here, I've adapted Marc's beautifully simple recipe for grilling on the panini press.

CHICKEN

2 tablespoons sake

2 tablespoons reduced-sodium soy sauce

2 tablespoons packed dark brown sugar

2 tablespoons mirin

4 boneless, skin-on chicken thighs (about 1 pound)

TERIYAKI SAUCE

2 tablespoons honey

2 tablespoons reduced-sodium soy sauce

2 tablespoons mirin

2 tablespoons sake

Toasted sesame seeds and chopped scallions, for garnish

Steamed rice, for serving

—

2 to 4 servings

CHICKEN: Mix the sake, soy sauce, brown sugar, and mirin in a small bowl until the sugar dissolves. Place the chicken in a zipper-top plastic bag and pour the marinade over the chicken. Seal the bag and roll the chicken around in the marinade to coat it. Let the chicken marinate in the refrigerator for 1 hour.

TERIYAKI SAUCE: While the chicken marinates, combine the honey, soy sauce, mirin, and sake in a small saucepan and bring to a boil over medium heat. Allow the sauce to simmer and reduce for a few minutes until it thickens slightly (it will not become especially thick). Remove it from the heat.

Heat the panini press to medium-high heat. If your panini press comes with a removable drip tray, make sure it is in place (see page 11).

Remove the chicken from the marinade (discard the remaining marinade) and pat it dry with paper towels. Grill the chicken, with the lid closed, until it's cooked to an internal temperature of 165°F and the skin is crispy, 6 to 8 minutes. Transfer the chicken to a serving platter and spoon some teriyaki sauce over the top. Garnish with toasted sesame seeds and chopped scallions and serve with steamed rice.

Citrus-Marinated Grilled Chicken

If you've ever wondered what makes the pollo asado, or grilled chicken, at Mexican restaurants so succulent and mouthwatering, the secret is often a citrus marinade. Lemons, limes, oranges—a good soak in their acidic juices makes chicken incredibly tender and flavorful. Serve it with warm tortillas, tomatoes, red onions, and cilantro. Consider grilling up a second batch—there should be enough remaining marinade—and then shred the chicken for No-Fuss, No-Flip Chicken Quesadillas (page 24).

¼ cup extra-virgin olive oil

Juice of 1 orange (about ¼ cup)

Juice of 1 lime (about 2 tablespoons)

Juice of 1 lemon (about 2 tablespoons)

¼ cup chopped fresh cilantro

2 garlic cloves, minced

1 serrano chile, seeded and minced

¼ teaspoon ground cumin

2 whole bone-in, skin-on chicken legs (drumstick and thigh), or 4 bone-in, skin-on chicken thighs (about 1½ pounds)

½ teaspoon coarse salt

¼ teaspoon freshly ground black pepper

Corn or flour tortillas, for serving

Chopped tomatoes, for serving

Chopped red onion, for serving

Fresh cilantro leaves, for serving

—

2 servings

Combine the oil, citrus juices, cilantro, garlic, chile, and cumin in a large zipper-top plastic bag. Add the chicken, seal the bag, and roll the chicken around a bit in the marinade to coat it well. Marinate the chicken in the refrigerator for 2 to 4 hours.

Heat the panini press to medium-high heat. If your panini press comes with a removable drip tray, make sure it is in place (see page 11).

Remove the chicken from the marinade, discarding the leftover marinade. Blot the excess liquid from the meat with paper towels and season both sides of the chicken with salt and pepper. Place the chicken on the grill, positioning it toward the center of the grill to ensure that the heat reaches all sides. Grill the chicken, with the lid closed, until it's cooked to an internal temperature of 165°F, 18 to 20 minutes.

Serve with warm tortillas and bowls of chopped tomatoes, chopped onions, and cilantro for tacos.

Grilled Jerk Chicken

If you've ever had jerk chicken, then you know what a powerful, spicy kick it has. If you haven't, you're in for a treat. Jerk spice originated in Jamaica and is rubbed onto everything from chicken to fish to tofu. Chicken, though, is probably the most popular jerk dish. What gives jerk its heat is the Scotch bonnet pepper, which is many times hotter than even a jalapeño (which is already pretty hot).

2 scallions, chopped

½ cup chopped red onion

3 garlic cloves, chopped

1 Scotch bonnet or habanero pepper, seeded and chopped (see Note)

2 tablespoons freshly squeezed lime juice

2 tablespoons reduced-sodium soy sauce

1 tablespoon extra-virgin olive oil

1 tablespoon packed brown sugar

2 teaspoons ground allspice

1 teaspoon chopped fresh thyme

½ teaspoon ground cinnamon

¼ teaspoon ground nutmeg

4 boneless, skinless chicken breasts (about 2 pounds)

Coarse salt and freshly ground black pepper

—
4 servings

Blend the scallions, red onion, garlic, Scotch bonnet pepper, lime juice, soy sauce, olive oil, brown sugar, allspice, thyme, cinnamon, and nutmeg in a blender or mini food processor until it forms a relatively smooth paste.

Season the chicken breasts with salt and pepper to taste and place them in a large zipper-top plastic bag. Pour the jerk paste over the chicken, seal the bag, and roll the chicken around in the paste to coat it. Let the chicken marinate in the refrigerator overnight.

Heat the panini press to medium-high heat. If your panini press comes with a removable drip tray, make sure it is in place (see page 11).

Using tongs, remove the chicken from the marinade (remember, there are hot peppers in there!) and transfer two chicken breasts to the grill.

Close the lid and grill the chicken breasts until they are cooked to an internal temperature of 165°F, 9 to 11 minutes. Transfer the chicken to a cutting board and let it rest for 5 to 10 minutes before serving. Meanwhile, cook the remaining two chicken breasts (and discard the remaining jerk paste). While the second batch of chicken is resting, unplug the grill and, while it's still hot, carefully scrape down the grates to remove any cooked-on jerk paste.

Brined Turkey Thigh

Last Thanksgiving at my in-laws' house, I saw a pan emerge from the oven, and I smiled with relief. They'd roasted an extra batch of turkey drumsticks and thighs. Hooray! No more having to scramble to the front of the line of family members to secure the ever-popular dark meat.

Unlike breasts and drumsticks, bone-in turkey thighs are well suited for grilling on a panini press due to their relatively flat shape. I love to first marinate the thighs overnight in an herb brine for lots of flavor. Don't wait till Thanksgiving to try this—it's great for dinner (with mashed potatoes and cranberry sauce and dressing) any time of the year. I often grill a second thigh while the first one is resting—there is enough brine to flavor two thighs—and slice it up for panini.

4 cups water

2 tablespoons coarse salt

1 tablespoons honey

1 teaspoon dried thyme

1 teaspoon dried sage

½ teaspoon dried rosemary

½ teaspoon freshly ground black pepper

1 (1-pound) bone-in, skin-on turkey thigh

1 tablespoon extra-virgin olive oil

—
2 servings

In a large bowl, stir together the water, salt, sugar, thyme, sage, rosemary, and black pepper until the salt and honey are dissolved. Submerge the turkey thigh in the brine (weight it with a small plate if necessary), cover the bowl with plastic wrap, and refrigerate for 2 to 3 hours.

Heat the panini press to medium-high heat. If your panini press comes with a removable drip tray, make sure it is in place (see page 11).

Remove the turkey thigh from the brine, pat it dry with paper towels, rub the skin side with the olive oil, and transfer it to the grill. Close the lid and grill the thigh until it is cooked to an internal temperature of 165°F, about 35 minutes.

Let the turkey rest for 10 minutes before serving.

Spatchcocked Game Hen

"Spatchcock" is a funny word, but it basically just means to butterfly. Removing the backbone of a chicken—or, in this case, a small game hen to fit on the panini press—and opening it up flat allows the bird to cook quickly and evenly. On a panini press, with heat from both sides, you can grill a game hen in under 20 minutes—about half the time it would take to roast it.

Game hens are often sold frozen, so be sure to allow plenty of time for yours to defrost in the refrigerator (it may take more than a day). This recipe is a very simple preparation, but you should always feel free to experiment with your favorite seasonings and spice rubs.

1 Cornish game hen (1½ to 2 pounds)

1 tablespoon extra-virgin olive oil

½ teaspoon coarse salt

¼ teaspoon freshly ground black pepper

—

2 servings

Heat the panini press to medium-high heat. If your panini press comes with a removable drip tray, make sure it is in place (see page 11).

Lay the game hen, breast side down, on a cutting board. With sturdy kitchen shears, cut through the ribs along both sides of the backbone, from tail to neck, to remove it (discard the backbone or save it to make chicken stock).

Open the hen out flat, still breast side down. Using a small paring knife, make a slice down the middle of the keel bone (the diamond-shaped white bone between the two breasts). Next, carefully cut around the thin, oblong strip of cartilage that runs down the middle of the hen. Once you've separated the cartilage from the flesh, reach in with your hands and lift it out and discard it. Don't worry if you're not able to do this as cleanly as you'd like—no one will notice.

Pat the hen dry and rub olive oil all over the bird. Season the hen on all sides with salt and pepper.

Carefully transfer the hen to the grill, skin side up, and close the lid. Grill the hen until it is cooked to an internal temperature of 165°F, 18 to 20 minutes.

Grilled Duck Breasts

I grilled duck breast after duck breast on my panini press, trying to figure out how to achieve that irresistible crispy skin everyone loves. Over and over again I got the same result—quickly cooked meat with a rubbery fat cap on top. Almost defeated, I was ready to put aside this idea and move on. But I had one duck breast left, and I went for a Hail Mary pass—cooking the duck, skin side down, with the grill open, hoping that this approach would give the duck a chance to render its fat without cooking the meat too fast. After about 9 minutes I peered under the duck to find what had been eluding me thus far: browned, crispy skin! I flipped the duck breast and closed the lid, and the other side finished cooking several minutes later. This, friends, was a triumphant moment in panini grilling.

2 boneless, skin-on duck breasts (about 12 ounces)

Coarse salt and freshly ground black pepper

—

4 servings

Heat the panini press to medium-low heat. If your panini press comes with a removable drip tray, make sure it is in place (see page 11).

Pat the duck breasts dry with a paper towel. With a sharp knife, score the fat layer on the duck breasts by carefully slicing through the skin just until you hit the meat (don't slice through the meat). Make several slices, about an inch apart, in a crosshatch pattern.

Season the duck generously on both sides with salt and pepper.

Open the panini press lid and lay one or both duck breasts on the grill (work in batches if only one will fit), skin side down. *Leaving the lid open,* grill the duck until much of the fat has rendered and the skin is brown and crispy, 9 to 11 minutes. Since grill temperatures vary, it may take more or less time for the duck to render its fat, crisp up, and brown on your grill. Using tongs, flip the breast(s) over and close the lid. Grill until the meat is cooked to an internal temperature of 150°F, another 3 to 4 minutes. Transfer the duck to a cutting board and allow it to rest for 10 minutes before slicing it across the grain.

NOTE:

If your panini press doesn't allow you to adjust the temperature, I wouldn't recommend using it to grill duck breasts. To render the duck's fat slowly, it's important to be able to cook it over lower heat— the default heat setting on a panini press without temperature adjustment may be too high to achieve this.

Grilled Duck Breast Salad with Fried Goat Cheese and Strawberries

This is one of my favorite springtime salads—panini-grilled duck breast, crunchy fried goat cheese medallions, and fresh strawberries over arugula, dressed in white balsamic vinaigrette. Don't you just love a salad with goodies all over the place? If you're not able to find duck, grilled chicken will work great here as well.

FRIED GOAT CHEESE

¼ cup panko bread crumbs

¼ cup plain bread crumbs

½ teaspoon coarse salt

¼ teaspoon freshly ground black pepper

¼ cup all-purpose flour

1 large egg, beaten

1 (5½-ounce) log goat cheese, sliced into ⅛-inch medallions (see Note)

3 tablespoons extra-virgin olive oil

SALAD

5 ounces baby arugula

1 cup sliced or quartered strawberries

1 recipe White Balsamic Vinaigrette (recipe follows)

2 Grilled Duck Breasts (page 35), sliced across the grain

—
4 servings

FRIED GOAT CHEESE: Combine the panko, plain breadcrumbs, salt, and pepper in a shallow bowl. Place the flour and beaten egg each in their own separate shallow bowls. Dredge each goat cheese medallion first in flour, then in egg, and lastly in the breadcrumbs.

In a medium-size skillet, heat the olive oil over medium heat. Carefully lower the cheese into the hot oil (be sure not to overcrowd the skillet—work in batches if necessary). Brown the cheese, 1 to 2 minutes per side, and drain the medallions on a paper towel.

SALAD: Place the arugula and strawberries in a large salad bowl. Pour vinaigrette over the salad—as much or as little as you'd like—and toss the salad with tongs.

To serve, divide the salad among four plates and top each with some fried goat cheese medallions and sliced duck breast.

NOTE:

An easy way to make nice, neat goat cheese slices is to cut them with a strand of unflavored dental floss; I keep a roll of floss in my utensil drawer just for this purpose! If you find that your goat cheese is too crumbly to slice, just let it sit out at room temperature for a few minutes.

White Balsamic Vinaigrette

I make a classic vinaigrette with white balsamic vinegar when I want to bring out the sweetness and acidity in ingredients like strawberries and tomatoes without adding the dark color of regular balsamic. Look for white balsamic at the grocery store next to the other vinegars.

3 tablespoons white balsamic vinegar (you can substitute regular balsamic)

2 teaspoons chopped shallots

½ teaspoon Dijon mustard

½ teaspoon coarse salt

½ teaspoon freshly ground black pepper

½ cup extra-virgin olive oil

—

About ¾ cup

In a small bowl, whisk together the vinegar, shallots, Dijon mustard, salt, and pepper. While still whisking, slowly drizzle in the olive oil.

You can keep any extra white balsamic vinaigrette in the refrigerator for up to a week. Allow the dressing to come to room temperature and give it a good stir before using it next.

CHAPTER 3

High on the Hog

Pork on the Panini Press

Spicy Elvis Panini

Peanut butter, bananas, and bacon—really? I avoided trying the famous Elvis sandwich for the longest time. It may have been a favorite of the King of Rock 'n' Roll, but that combination just didn't scream "Love Me Tender" to me. That is, until the day my friend Amanda introduced me to a new twist on peanut butter: spicy. She had mixed sriracha—a Thai hot pepper sauce—into peanut butter and slathered it on bread and could not contain her excitement over her culinary discovery. Suddenly I began to look at peanut butter with new eyes and new possibilities . . . possibilities that could allow the inclusion of bananas and bacon.

Oh all right, I loved it. And I think you will, too, especially if you go for ripe, sweet bananas—perfectly yellow with a little bite to them, not mushy. It's completely up to you just how spicy to make things, but that little kick of heat in combination with the sweet, salty, and smoky flavors in this sandwich is definitely enough to get your taste buds "All Shook Up."

½ cup creamy or chunky peanut butter

½ to 1 teaspoon sriracha or other hot pepper sauce

4 tablespoons (½ stick) butter, at room temperature

8 slices rustic white bread, sliced from a dense bakery loaf

2 ripe bananas, thinly sliced

8 strips cooked bacon

—

4 panini

Heat the panini press to medium-high heat.

Mix the peanut butter and sriracha in a small bowl until well combined.

FOR EACH SANDWICH: Spread butter on two slices of bread to flavor the outside of the sandwich. Flip over both slices and spread 1 tablespoon spicy peanut butter on each. Top one slice of bread with sliced bananas and 2 bacon strips. Close the sandwich with the other slice of bread, buttered side up.

Grill two panini at a time, with the lid closed, until the ingredients are warmed through and the bread is toasted, 2 to 3 minutes.

Manchego, Honey, and Hot Soppressata Panini

One spring afternoon on a visit to San Francisco, my husband, Mike, our friend Alissa, and I perched ourselves on the high stools at Blue Barn Gourmet in the city's Marina district and eagerly unwrapped several of their grilled cheese sandwich offerings. Mike's selection, known as the Sheep, was our hands-down favorite—Manchego (my favorite cheese), spicy salami, and fig jam on levain. The sweet heat of the salami combined with the buttery Manchego was just out of this world. I couldn't wait to get home and make some of my own. I replaced the fig jam with some floral honey, which I just love with salami.

4 tablespoons (½ stick) butter, at room temperature

8 slices rustic white bread, sliced from a dense bakery loaf

4 teaspoons honey

8 ounces Manchego cheese, thinly sliced

8 ounces sliced hot soppressata

—
4 panini

Heat the panini press to medium-high heat.

FOR EACH SANDWICH: Spread butter on two slices of bread to flavor the outside of the sandwich. Flip over both slices and drizzle honey on the other side of each. On one slice layer cheese, soppressata, and more cheese. Close the sandwich with the other slice of bread, buttered side up.

Grill two panini at a time, with the lid closed, until the cheese is melted and the bread is toasted, 4 to 5 minutes.

Salami, Taleggio, and Peach Panini

If there's a specialty cheese shop near you—or even a specialty cheese section of your regular grocery store—start chatting up the folks behind the counter for their recommendations. Tasting different cheeses is undoubtedly the best way to learn about cheese. It's how I first learned about Taleggio. Someone behind the counter gave me a sample of the Italian cow's milk cheese along with a slice of salami. It was love at first bite. Taleggio's aroma is on the strong side, but its flavor is comparatively mild—with a hint of fruitiness that pairs well with sweet peaches. Fontina, another easy-melting cow's milk cheese with a nutty and somewhat fruity flavor, is a good substitute and tends to be easier to find in stores.

1 tablespoon extra-virgin olive oil

8 slices whole-grain bread, sliced from a dense bakery loaf

½ cup pesto, purchased or homemade (page 45)

4 ounces Taleggio cheese, rind removed, sliced

4 ounces Genoa salami, sliced

1 medium-size peach, pitted and sliced

—

4 panini

Heat the panini press to medium-high heat.

FOR EACH SANDWICH: Brush olive oil on two slices of bread to flavor the outside of the sandwich. Flip over both slices of bread and spread pesto on the other side of each. On one slice layer cheese, salami, peach slices, and more cheese. Close the sandwich with the other slice of bread, oiled side up.

Grill two panini at a time, with the lid closed, until the cheese is melted and the bread is toasted, 4 to 5 minutes.

Pesto

Pesto is one of the most flavorful condiments I can think of. It instantly adds a fresh, zesty, garlicky punch to panini, as well as pasta, pizzas, and many other dishes. You can find jars of pesto at the grocery store, but it's easy enough to make at home. Plus, if you make it yourself you're able to increase or decrease ingredient quantities according to your preferences. Pesto can be made with a variety of different herbs. Basil pesto is probably the most common form, but I've also included instructions for a lemony arugula pesto.

2 large garlic cloves

⅓ cup pine nuts

2 cups fresh basil leaves

⅔ cup extra-virgin olive oil

⅔ cup grated Parmesan or Pecorino Romano cheese

Coarse salt and freshly ground black pepper

—

About 1¼ cups

Using a blender or food processor, blend the garlic and pine nuts for a few seconds until they're the texture of coarse meal. Add the basil leaves. Continue to blend, drizzling in the olive oil through the feed tube, until the pesto is completely pureed. Add the cheese and blend until it's fully mixed in.

Transfer the pesto to a small bowl, taste it, and season with salt and pepper as needed.

Store the pesto for up to 5 days in the refrigerator or up to 2 months in the freezer. Cover the pesto with a thin layer of olive oil to help preserve its bright green color.

FOR ARUGULA PESTO: Substitute ⅓ cup chopped walnuts for the pine nuts and 2 cups baby arugula for the basil. Blend in 1 tablespoon grated lemon zest and 1 tablespoon freshly squeezed lemon juice along with the cheese.

Pepperoni Pizza Panini

Of all the panini ideas that people have suggested to me—it tends to be a popular topic of conversation—Pepperoni Pizza Panini is probably the most common. I'm not quite sure why that is. I'm guessing it's because it was a rather obvious omission from my blog for the longest time. Honestly, I didn't think it was worth posting a recipe for something that everyone in America knows how to make—pepperoni, cheese, sauce, and bread is very standard fare.

But it turns out that these aren't quite as straightforward as I thought. You see, if you spread marinara sauce directly on sliced bread or a roll, as I typically do with most panini condiments, the bread turns soggy. And that's not good. After some trial and error I discovered a solution: flatbread. Sauce doesn't seep into flatbreads like naan or pita as easily as it does with cut sides of other breads. Plus, with its crust-like texture, it feels like you're eating a folded pizza. Come to think of it, I would have viewed folding a slice of cold leftover pizza and popping it into the panini press as a very viable reheating method back in my college days.

4 flatbreads, such as naan or pita

½ cup marinara sauce

8 ounces fresh mozzarella cheese, sliced

4 ounces sliced pepperoni

8 fresh basil leaves, torn

—

4 panini

Heat the panini press to medium-high heat.

FOR EACH SANDWICH: Cut the flatbread in half across the diameter, creating two semicircles—these will become your top and bottom halves. Spread a layer of marinara on both flatbread halves. Top one half with a thin layer of cheese and arrange pepperoni slices to cover the cheese. Scatter some basil pieces over the pepperoni and top with more cheese. Close the sandwich with the other flatbread half, marinara side down.

Grill two panini at a time, with the lid closed, until the cheese is melted and the bread is toasted, 5 to 6 minutes.

Chorizo Tortas

My taste buds immediately perk up when I see that Mexican chorizo is an ingredient in a dish. I just love that combination of chile and vinegar flavors. In these tortas (Mexican sandwiches) I layer ground chorizo with refried beans and top them with avocado, red onions, and queso fresco on traditional telera rolls.

You'll need uncooked Mexican chorizo for these sandwiches. It's soft, minced, and deep red in color from a good amount of chiles. It's not the same as Spanish chorizo, which is hard and dry-cured—another delicious sausage for another day.

10 ounces uncooked Mexican chorizo (not dry-cured)

½ cup refried beans (see Note)

4 *bolillo* or *telera* rolls (kaiser rolls will work well, too)

1 medium-size ripe avocado, pitted, peeled, and sliced

½ small red onion, sliced

2 ounces crumbled queso fresco (or mild feta cheese)

—

4 tortas

Place the chorizo in a large skillet over medium heat. Cook the chorizo, breaking it up with a wooden spoon, until it's cooked through, about 10 minutes. Use a slotted spoon to transfer the cooked chorizo to a plate lined with paper towels to drain the excess fat.

While the chorizo is cooking, heat the refried beans in a small saucepan over medium heat, stirring occasionally.

Heat the panini press to medium-high heat.

FOR EACH SANDWICH: Split a roll to create top and bottom halves. Spread 2 tablespoons refried beans inside the bottom half of the roll. Top the beans with chorizo, avocado, red onions, and *queso fresco*. Close the sandwich with the top half of the roll.

Grill two tortas at a time, with the lid closed, until the rolls are toasted, 4 to 5 minutes.

NOTE:

Refried beans typically come canned in a larger quantity than you'll need for this recipe. What to do with the remaining beans? You could use them in Grilled Steak Tortas (page 60) or swap them for the mashed black beans in Grilled Shrimp Tostadas (page 82). If you store the beans in a covered glass or plastic container, they'll keep in the refrigerator for 3 to 4 days.

Grilled Bacon

You won't believe how easy it is to grill bacon on a panini press. It takes less time than frying or baking, and it's the perfect option on hot summer days when you don't want to stand over a stove or turn on the oven.

6 strips uncooked bacon

—
6 strips

Heat the panini press to medium-high heat. If your panini press comes with a removable drip tray, make sure it is in place (see page 11).

Arrange as many bacon slices as will fit neatly on your grill, without overlapping. Depending on the size of your grill, you may need to trim the bacon to fit.

If you have a grill that allows you to adjust the height of the upper plate, set it to just barely graze the surface of bacon and not fully press the strips. Close the lid and grill the bacon until it's cooked through and crispy, 10 to 13 minutes, depending on the thickness of your bacon.

Beer-Grilled Bratwursts

Don't let rain put a damper on your sports watching (and eating) plans. Grill your brats inside on the panini press. Actually, you'll only be finishing the sausages on the grill—the main cooking will happen in a pot full of beer and onions on the stove. While the bratwursts simmer and soak in all that great flavor, grill some onions on the panini press. Then crisp up the brats on the grill—you won't even need to turn them.

Beyond bratwurst, you can grill pretty much any precooked sausage on the panini press—hot dogs, chicken sausages, breakfast links, you name it. The key is to keep the heat on the lower side to avoid bursting the casings. If your panini press doesn't allow you to adjust the heat, you may want to test it out on just one sausage at first.

2 tablespoons butter

2 medium-size onions

4 uncooked bratwursts (about 1 pound)

2 to 3 (12-ounce) bottles or cans beer (see Note)

1 teaspoon vegetable oil

4 bratwurst buns or hot dog buns, toasted if desired

1 cup sauerkraut

German-style or Dijon mustard, to taste

—

4 servings

Melt the butter in a Dutch oven or large pot over medium-high heat. Halve and slice one of the onions, add the slices to the pot, and cook, stirring occasionally, until they're softened, 4 to 5 minutes. Add the bratwursts and enough beer to cover them. Bring the beer to a boil, then immediately reduce the heat to a simmer. Continue cooking the bratwursts for another 10 minutes (if the total weight of your bratwursts is more than a pound, cook them for an extra few minutes—but not too much longer, as you don't want to overcook these). They will feel denser to the touch when they're done—don't slice into them or all of the juices will escape!

While the bratwursts are simmering, heat the panini press to medium-high heat. Slice the remaining onion crosswise into ½-inch-thick rounds, keeping the rings intact. Brush vegetable oil over both sides of the onion rounds and grill them, with the lid closed, until they're tender and grill marks appear, 4 to 6 minutes. Transfer the onions to a plate.

Reduce the heat on the panini press to medium-low (if the heat is too high it may cause the bratwurst skin to burst). With a pair of tongs, remove the bratwursts from the beer, set them on the panini press, and close the lid. Grill the bratwursts until dark grill marks appear, 4 to 5 minutes.

Serve the bratwursts on buns with grilled onions, sauerkraut, and mustard.

Sweet and Smoky Grilled Pork Tenderloin Medallions

True to its name, this recipe is sweet and smoky—and extremely easy to prepare on a weeknight. I make a quick spice paste, starring brown sugar and smoked paprika, and let it soak into the pork while I prepare a simple side dish. Then, after just 2 minutes on the panini press, the meat is juicy, flavorful . . . and done!

1 tablespoon packed brown sugar

1 teaspoon coarse salt

1 teaspoon smoked paprika

¼ teaspoon dry mustard

¼ teaspoon garlic powder

¼ teaspoon freshly ground black pepper

A dash of cayenne pepper

2 teaspoons vegetable oil

1 (1-pound) pork tenderloin

—
4 servings

In a small bowl, mix the brown sugar, salt, smoked paprika, dry mustard, garlic powder, black pepper, and cayenne until they're well combined. Stir in the vegetable oil to form a paste.

Cut the pork tenderloin crosswise into 8 pieces, each about 1 inch thick. Use the heel of your hand to press each piece into a ½-inch-thick medallion.

Rub ¼ to ½ teaspoon of the spice paste over the top and bottom of each pork medallion. Let the pork sit at room temperature for 30 minutes to allow the flavors to seep in.

Heat the panini press to high heat. If your panini press comes with a removable drip tray, make sure it is in place (see page 11).

Working in batches if necessary, place the pork medallions on the grill and close the lid. Grill the pork until it's cooked to an internal temperature of 145°F, about 2 minutes. Allow the pork to rest for 5 minutes before slicing.

CHAPTER 4

The Butcher's Best

Beef and Lamb on the Panini Press

Hawaiian Flank Steak Teriyaki Panini

Believe it or not, I built these panini around the sweet Maui onions rather than the steak. Just the thought of Maui onions takes me right back to my honeymoon and Kula Lodge, the dark wood restaurant perched on a hillside in the island's upcountry, where they served my husband and me Maui onion soup—with a side of sweeping views of the Pacific. To bring these nostalgia-inducing onions into my sandwiches, I fry them nice and crispy and, in keeping with the Hawaiian mood, match them with teriyaki-marinated flank steak, grilled pineapple, cilantro, and teriyaki mayonnaise. Since there's no cheese to melt on these panini, I simply toast the bread on the panini press rather than grill the sandwiches.

MARINATED FLANK STEAK

3 tablespoons mirin

3 tablespoons reduced-sodium soy sauce

3 tablespoons sake

1 tablespoon packed dark brown sugar

2 teaspoons grated fresh ginger

1 (1- to 1½-pound) flank steak

TERIYAKI MAYONNAISE

½ cup mayonnaise

1 tablespoon reduced-sodium soy sauce

1 tablespoon mirin

1 teaspoon grated fresh ginger

PANINI

1 ciabatta loaf, cut into 4 portions, or 4 ciabatta rolls

8 pineapple rings, canned or fresh, patted dry with paper towels

¼ cup chopped fresh cilantro

1 recipe Crispy Fried Onions (page 58)

—

4 panini

MARINATED FLANK STEAK: Whisk together the mirin, soy sauce, sake, dark brown sugar, and ginger in a small bowl until the sugar has dissolved. Place the flank steak in a large zipper-top plastic bag and pour in the marinade. Seal the bag and rotate the steak around a bit to make sure the marinade fully coats it. Marinate the steak in the refrigerator for at least 4 hours and up to 24 hours.

TERIYAKI MAYONNAISE: In a small bowl, whisk together the mayonnaise, soy sauce, mirin, and ginger until well combined and smooth. Refrigerate the mayonnaise until you're ready to use it.

PANINI: Heat the panini press to medium-high heat.

Grill two ciabatta portions at a time, cut sides down, until they're toasted and grill marks appear, about 2 minutes. Set aside.

Grill the pineapple slices, in batches if necessary, until they're caramelized and dark grill marks appear, 3 to 4 minutes. Carefully scrape the excess pineapple juices from the grates with a grill scraper.

Raise the heat on the panini press to high. If your panini press comes with a removable drip tray, make sure it is in place (see page 11).

(continued)

Remove the flank steak from the plastic bag, discarding the marinade. Place the steak on the grill, close the lid, and grill the steak to your desired doneness, 8 to 10 minutes for medium (137°F). Allow the steak to rest on a cutting board for 10 minutes before slicing it thinly across the grain. Meanwhile, unplug the grill and, while it's still hot, carefully scrape down the grates with your grill scraper to remove any stuck-on bits of meat.

FOR EACH SANDWICH: Spread 1 tablespoon teriyaki mayonnaise on the cut sides of a toasted ciabatta portion. On the bottom half, lay 2 pineapple rings, some steak, a sprinkling of chopped cilantro, and some fried onions. Close the panini with the top ciabatta half.

Crispy Fried Onions

I wish I didn't love these onions so much. By the time the last batch is done, I've often already polished off the first batch! Snacking aside, these crispy onions are perfect for adding a savory crunch to beef and vegetable panini or as a garnish for dishes like Grilled Rib-Eye Steak (page 73) or Grilled Salmon with Old Bay Aioli (page 86).

½ cup vegetable oil

½ cup all-purpose flour

½ teaspoon coarse salt

1 sweet onion (such as Maui, Walla Walla, or Vidalia), halved and thinly sliced

—

About 1 cup

Heat the vegetable oil in a medium-size skillet over medium-high heat until a pinch of flour sizzles on contact.

Combine the flour and salt in a shallow bowl and toss the onions around in the mixture until they're well coated. Carefully add the onions to the hot oil—in batches if necessary to avoid overcrowding the pan—and cook them, stirring occasionally, until they are golden brown and crisp, 4 to 5 minutes. Use a slotted spoon to transfer the onions to a plate lined with paper towels to drain.

Chimichurri Skirt Steak Panini with Provolone and Sun-Dried Tomatoes

Once you've tried steak with chimichurri sauce, it's a natural inclination to want to make a sandwich out of it. Not only do the tender slices of steak combine beautifully with sharp melted cheese, but the zesty, garlicky Argentine sauce is a real treat when it soaks into bread. Here, I've chosen to use a sturdy French baguette that can absorb all of that sauce without sacrificing its firm texture. A few sun-dried tomatoes scattered over the top bring a sweet burst to each bite.

1 French baguette, cut into 4 portions, or 4 mini baguettes

½ cup Chimichurri Sauce (page 71)

1 recipe Chimichurri Skirt Steak (page 70)

¼ cup thinly sliced oil-packed sun-dried tomatoes

4 ounces provolone cheese, sliced

—
4 panini

Heat the panini press to medium-high heat.

FOR EACH SANDWICH: Slice off the domed top of a baguette portion to create a flat grilling surface. Split the baguette to create top and bottom halves. Spoon 1 tablespoon chimichurri sauce inside each half. On the bottom half layer steak, sun-dried tomatoes, and cheese. Close the sandwich with the top baguette half.

Grill two panini at a time, with the lid closed, until the cheese is melted and the baguettes are toasted, 5 to 7 minutes.

USE LEFTOVERS: You can make these panini with any leftover steak you have on hand, and substitute pesto (purchased or homemade, page 45) for the chimichurri sauce.

Grilled Steak Tortas

This recipe calls for cumin-grilled flatiron steak and rajas (grilled red bell peppers, poblanos, and onions) for you to turn into Mexican steak tortas, but in reality these hearty grilled sandwiches are an excellent way to use up any leftover meat or chicken you might have on hand. You just split a sandwich roll, spread on some refried beans, and then top them with meat, cheese, rajas, and any other toppings you like.

STEAK

1 (1-pound) flatiron or top blade steak

1 teaspoon coarse salt

1 teaspoon garlic powder

½ teaspoon ground cumin

½ teaspoon freshly ground black pepper

TORTAS

½ cup refried beans

4 *bolillo* or *telera* rolls (kaiser rolls will also work well)

1 recipe *Rajas* (page 75)

1 medium-size ripe avocado, pitted, peeled, and sliced

4 ounces pepper Jack cheese, sliced

—

4 tortas

STEAK: Heat the panini press to high heat. If your panini press comes with a removable drip tray, make sure it is in place (see page 11).

Season both sides of the steak with salt, garlic powder, cumin, and pepper. Grill the steak, with the lid closed, to your desired doneness, 5 to 7 minutes for medium (137°F).

Transfer the steak to a cutting board and let it rest for 10 minutes before slicing it very thinly across the grain. Meanwhile, unplug the grill and, while it's still hot, carefully scrape down the grates with a grill scraper to remove any stuck-on bits of meat.

TORTAS: Reheat the panini press to medium-high heat. Heat the refried beans in a small saucepan over medium heat, stirring occasionally.

FOR EACH SANDWICH: Split a roll to create top and bottom halves. Spread 2 tablespoons refried beans on the bottom half of the roll. Top it with steak, *rajas*, avocado, and cheese. Close the sandwich with the top half of the roll.

Grill two tortas at a time, with the lid closed, until the cheese is melted and the rolls are toasted, 4 to 5 minutes.

Green Chile Steak Melt Panini

At the end of a long day of kite flying and butterfly chasing on a family vacation in Santa Barbara, I ordered a fantastic spicy steak sandwich at a restaurant that evening. It was a Southwestern take on the classic cheese steak, made with thinly sliced steak, chiles, onions, pepper Jack cheese, and chipotle crema on a baguette. The concept went straight into the Notes app on my iPhone to remind me to re-create it when I got back home. For my version, I caramelized the onions to bring in more sweetness and dialed down the spice level a touch by using Monterey Jack rather than pepper Jack. Lastly, I converted the chipotle crema to a chipotle mayonnaise (which still has a touch of cooling sour cream in it).

1 (1-pound) New York strip steak

Coarse salt and freshly ground black pepper

1 ciabatta loaf, cut into 4 portions, or 4 ciabatta rolls

1 recipe Chipotle Mayonnaise (recipe follows)

4 ounces Monterey Jack cheese, sliced

1 cup Caramelized Onions (page 19)

1 (7-ounce) can roasted whole green chiles, drained and chopped

—
4 panini

Heat the panini press to high heat. If your panini press comes with a removable drip tray, make sure it is in place (see page 11).

Season the steak generously with salt and pepper.

Grill the steak, with the lid closed, to your desired doneness, 10 to 15 minutes for medium (137°F). Transfer the steak to a cutting board and let it rest for 10 minutes before slicing it very thinly across the grain. Meanwhile, unplug the grill and, while it's still hot, scrape down the grates with a grill scraper. Let the grill cool, and clean the grates.

Reheat the panini press to medium-high heat.

FOR EACH SANDWICH: Split the ciabatta to create top and bottom halves. Spread 1 tablespoon chipotle mayonnaise inside each half. On the bottom half layer cheese, steak, onions, chiles, and more cheese. Close the sandwich with the top half.

Grill two panini at a time, with the lid closed, until the cheese is melted and the rolls are toasted, 5 to 7 minutes.

USE LEFTOVERS: If you've got leftover steak on hand, go ahead and use it here instead of grilling a new steak.

(continued)

Chipotle Mayonnaise

Get ready for a Southwestern kick! Smoky chipotle peppers (which are ripe jalapeños that have been smoke-dried) bring fiery flavor to this spread, which I adore on everything from steak to turkey to salmon. The sour cream cools things off, keeping the spice level in check. If you find it too hot for your taste, just add more sour cream.

½ cup mayonnaise

1 tablespoon sour cream

1 tablespoon finely chopped chives

1 canned chipotle in adobo sauce, plus 1½ teaspoons of the adobo sauce

1 teaspoon freshly squeezed lemon juice

Coarse salt and freshly ground black pepper

—
About ½ cup

Combine the mayonnaise, sour cream, chives, chipotle, adobo sauce, and lemon juice in a food processor or blender. Process or blend until smooth. Season the mayonnaise with salt and pepper to taste. Cover the bowl and refrigerate the mayonnaise until you are ready to serve it.

Meatloaf Melt Panini

Out of all the panini that I make from leftovers, these set themselves apart in an important way: a built-in condiment. It's the ketchup—or barbecue sauce or marinara, or whatever sauce you might have chosen to top your meatloaf. Each slice comes with its own strip of sauce, so all you need to add is cheese, onions, and bread, and you've got a perfect sandwich.

As an aside, can you think about meatloaf without hearing Will Ferrell hollering "MA! THE MEATLOAF!!" as Chazz in the movie Wedding Crashers? Neither can I.

4 tablespoons (½ stick) butter, at room temperature

8 slices rye or other rustic bread, sliced from a dense bakery loaf

1 cup Caramelized Onions (page 19)

4 thick slices leftover meatloaf, preferably with a topping like ketchup

4 ounces Swiss or sharp cheddar cheese, sliced

—
4 panini

Heat the panini press to medium-high heat.

FOR EACH SANDWICH: Spread butter on two slices of bread to flavor the outside of the sandwich. Flip over one slice of bread and top it with caramelized onions, a slice of meatloaf, and cheese. Close the sandwich with the other slice of bread, buttered side up.

Grill two panini at a time, with the lid closed, until the cheese is melted and the bread is toasted, 4 to 5 minutes.

California Steak Panini

There is a San Diego food specialty that the tourist guidebooks probably won't tell you about. You can get it at one place only, and you actually have to cook it yourself. It's the burgundy pepper tri-tip—affectionately dubbed "Cardiff Crack" by those in the know—at Seaside Market in Cardiff-by-the-Sea. Bathing an already flavorful cut of beef in a bold marinade is bound to get you some notice. It's no surprise that they don't publicize the recipe, or I'd tell you what was in it. The best way I can describe it is that it tastes just like a really great steak, only better.

I call these California Steak Panini because each of the ingredients is particularly beloved in my home state. I usually make them with leftover marinated tri-tip from Seaside Market, but this simple salt-and-pepper steak works great, too.

TRI-TIP

1 (1½-pound) tri-tip steak

1 teaspoon coarse salt

½ teaspoon freshly ground black pepper

PANINI

4 tablespoons Chipotle Mayonnaise (page 62) or purchased plain mayonnaise

4 sourdough rolls

1 medium-size ripe avocado, pitted, peeled, and sliced

8 Slow-Roasted Tomato halves (recipe follows) or oil-packed sun-dried tomatoes

4 ounces Monterey Jack or pepper Jack cheese, sliced

—

4 panini

TRI-TIP: Heat the panini press to medium-high heat. If your panini press comes with a removable drip tray, make sure it is in place (see page 11).

Season the steak with salt and pepper. Set the steak on the grill, close the lid, and grill to your desired doneness, 20 to 22 minutes for medium (137°F).

Transfer the steak to a cutting board and allow it to rest for at least 10 minutes before slicing it thinly across the grain. You can either clean off your grill at this point or take advantage of the extra flavor those leftover juices will add to your panini when it comes time to grill them.

Reheat the panini press to medium-high heat.

FOR EACH SANDWICH: Split a roll to create top and bottom halves. Spread 1 tablespoon chipotle mayonnaise inside the bottom half. Layer on avocado slices, steak, 2 tomato halves, and cheese. Close the sandwich with the top half of the roll.

Grill two panini at a time, with the lid closed, until the cheese is melted and the rolls are toasted, 5 to 7 minutes.

Slow-Roasted Tomatoes

Even sweeter than fresh tomatoes and plumper than sun-dried ones, roasted tomatoes bring big, juicy bursts of flavor to everything from panini to pasta to pizzas. Just let them bake away in a low oven for several hours, all the while filling your kitchen with marinara-like aromas. I adapted this simple method from the Smitten Kitchen blog.

12 plum tomatoes (such as Roma), halved lengthwise

Extra-virgin olive oil

Coarse salt and freshly ground black pepper

—

24 halves

Heat the oven to 225°F. Arrange the tomato halves, cut sides up, on a parchment-lined baking sheet. Drizzle the tomatoes lightly with olive oil and season them with salt and pepper. Use a light hand with the seasoning, as the tomatoes will be naturally very flavorful once they are roasted.

Roast the tomatoes in the oven until they are shriveled and mostly dry, 3 to 4 hours.

Use the tomatoes immediately or allow them to cool, cover them with more olive oil, and store them in the refrigerator for sandwiches, pasta, pizzas, or just snacking over the next several days.

Cheeseburger Patty Melt Panini

I might go so far as to say that a patty melt is even better than a regular burger. Grilled on rye bread and enveloped in cheese, a patty melt tends to hold its ingredients intact better than its burger counterpart. Condiments like grilled onions and Thousand Island dressing are an insurance policy, so that on the off chance you overcook the patty, you'll still end up with a flavorful sandwich. And then there's the rye bread—bread that actually tastes like something—cradling your burger patty. Yup, give me a good patty melt over a regular burger any day.

1 tablespoon vegetable oil

1 medium-size onion, sliced into ½-inch-thick rounds (rings intact)

1 pound 85% lean ground beef

1 teaspoon coarse salt

½ teaspoon freshly ground black pepper

4 tablespoons (½ stick) butter, at room temperature

8 slices rye bread or rustic white bread, sliced from a dense bakery loaf

4 ounces sharp cheddar or Swiss cheese, sliced

1 recipe Thousand Island Dressing (page 68)

—

4 panini

Heat the panini press to medium-high heat. If your panini press comes with a removable drip tray, make sure it is in place (see page 11).

Brush vegetable oil on both sides of the onions. Grill the onions until they're tender and dark grill marks appear, 6 to 8 minutes. Transfer the grilled onions to a plate.

While the onions are grilling, divide the ground beef into four equal patties. Season the patties on both sides with salt and pepper. After the onions are cooked, grill the burgers to your desired doneness, 4 to 5 minutes for medium (137°F). Carefully scrape the grates with a grill scraper to remove most of the excess grease and cooked-on bits (they don't need to be completely clean).

FOR EACH SANDWICH: Spread butter on two slices of bread to flavor the outside of the sandwich. Flip over one slice and top the other side with cheese, grilled onions, a burger patty, a dollop of Thousand Island dressing, and more cheese. Close the sandwich with the other slice of bread, buttered side up.

Grill two panini at a time, with the lid closed, until the cheese is melted and the bread is toasted, 4 to 5 minutes.

Reuben Panini

Once upon a time I asked Panini Happy readers to name their favorite sandwich. The overwhelming choice turned out to be the Reuben. It wasn't hard for me to understand why. Just the sight of all of that bright pink, salty corned beef piled on top of mouthwatering sauerkraut, with Thousand Island dressing and melted Swiss cheese on rye . . . well, you know you're in for a flavor explosion.

4 tablespoons (½ stick) butter, at room temperature

8 slices rye bread, sliced from a dense bakery loaf

4 ounces Swiss cheese, sliced

8 ounces sliced corned beef

1 recipe Thousand Island Dressing (recipe follows)

½ cup sauerkraut

—

4 panini

There are lots of Reuben variations out there—some use turkey or pastrami instead of corned beef, some opt for Russian dressing rather than Thousand Island. This version happens to be the one I like best, especially after St. Patrick's Day, when there is leftover corned beef in the fridge.

Heat the panini press to medium-high heat.

FOR EACH SANDWICH: Spread butter on two slices of bread to flavor the outside of the sandwich. Flip over one slice and top the other side with cheese, corned beef, a dollop of Thousand Island dressing, sauerkraut, and more cheese. Close the sandwich with the other slice of bread, buttered side up.

Grill two panini at a time, with the lid closed, until the cheese is melted and the bread is toasted, 4 to 5 minutes.

Thousand Island Dressing

Classic Thousand Island dressing is good for more than just an iceberg lettuce salad. Use this creamy, tangy condiment for everything from a spread for burgers and turkey sandwiches to a dip for shrimp.

½ cup mayonnaise

2 tablespoons ketchup

2 teaspoons sweet pickle relish

2 teaspoons Worcestershire sauce

2 teaspoons minced onion

Coarse salt and freshly ground black pepper

—

About ½ cup

Whisk together the mayonnaise, ketchup, pickle relish, Worcestershire sauce, and onion in a small bowl, and season with salt and pepper to taste. Cover the bowl and refrigerate the dressing until you're ready to use it.

Chimichurri Skirt Steak

I've chosen to dress this simple grilled skirt steak in chimichurri sauce, but you can always take the same steak, add your own favorite seasonings, and use it in tacos, salads, or, of course, sandwiches. You may want to double the recipe to make Chimichurri Skirt Steak Panini with Provolone and Sun-Dried Tomatoes (page 59) later in the week.

1 (1-pound) skirt steak (see Note)

Coarse salt and freshly ground black pepper

1 recipe Chimichurri Sauce (recipe follows)

—

2 to 4 servings

NOTE:

You might be able to find skirt steak in the butcher department of your regular grocery store; if not, look for it at a specialty grocer or butcher shop. Alternatively, you can substitute flank steak for this recipe.

About 30 minutes before you're ready to grill, set the steak out at room temperature. If necessary, trim the length of the steak strips to fit your grill.

Heat the panini press to high heat. If your panini press comes with a removable drip tray, make sure it is in place (see page 11).

Pat the steak dry with paper towels, season it generously with salt and pepper, and place it on the grill. Close the lid so that the upper plate is resting on the meat.

Grill the steak until it's cooked to your desired doneness, 4 to 5 minutes for medium (137°F).

Let the steak rest for 5 minutes before slicing it thinly across the grain, with your knife set at a 45° angle (this will give you really tender slices). Serve the steak with the chimichurri sauce.

Chimichurri Sauce

The first time I ever tried chimichurri sauce I was blown away by how much fresh, herby, garlicky flavor was packed inside it. The sauce, which originated in Argentina, reminds me a bit of pesto, minus the creaminess. It's the kind of stuff that makes you start looking around your fridge and pantry for all kinds of ways to use it—bread to drizzle it on, potatoes to toss it in for a salad, vegetables to marinate in it. You don't want a single drop of this to go to waste.

1 cup packed finely chopped fresh Italian parsley

4 garlic cloves, minced

½ cup extra-virgin olive oil

1 tablespoon red wine vinegar

1 tablespoon freshly squeezed lemon juice

1 tablespoon dried oregano

1 teaspoon coarse salt

¼ teaspoon freshly ground black pepper

¼ teaspoon red pepper flakes

—

About ¾ cup

Combine all of the ingredients in a medium nonreactive bowl and set the sauce aside at room temperature until ready to use. You can store any leftover chimichurri sauce in an airtight container in the refrigerator for a day or two—just bring it back to room temperature before you serve it.

Grilled Rib-Eye Steak

Most often I grill with big-flavor marinades, but once in a while I yearn for the simplicity of the salt-and-pepper-only route. Especially when I've got a thick, wonderfully marbled cut of meat like a rib-eye, I want the natural richness of the meat to really shine through.

1 (1¼-pound) rib-eye steak, about 1½ inches thick

1 tablespoon extra-virgin olive oil

Freshly ground black pepper

Coarse salt

—

2 servings

Pat the steak dry with paper towels, rub olive oil all over it, and season it generously with black pepper. Set it out at room temperature for about 30 minutes.

Heat the panini press to high heat. If your panini press comes with a removable drip tray, make sure it is in place (see page 11).

Season the steak generously with coarse salt and set it on the grill. Close the lid so that it's resting right on top of the meat. Don't bother adjusting the height of the upper plate (if your grill has that feature). The steak will shrink a little as it cooks, and if your grill height is in a fixed position it will likely lose contact with the meat.

Grill the steak to your desired doneness, 12 to 15 minutes for medium (137°F). If your steak happens to weigh more or less than 1¼ pounds, just adjust your grilling time. I can't underscore enough how helpful an instant-read thermometer is for grilling to the right temperature.

Let the steak rest for 10 minutes on a cutting board before slicing it thinly across the grain.

Rajas, Steak, and Egg Panini

If you're looking for a lighter, healthier, simpler breakfast sandwich option, this ain't it—flip on over to the Egg White Omelet Panino (page 100) instead. These take some time to prepare, and they're hardly light—but they're fabulous. They're the ultimate steak and egg panini—cumin-grilled flat-iron steak, rajas (grilled red bell peppers, poblanos, and onions), an omelet, and sharp cheddar on sourdough. If cowboys ate panini, I could picture them going for these.

STEAK

1 (1-pound) flatiron or top blade steak

1 teaspoon coarse salt

1 teaspoon garlic powder

½ teaspoon ground cumin

½ teaspoon freshly ground black pepper

OMELETS

2 teaspoons butter

4 large eggs

Coarse salt and freshly ground black pepper

PANINI

4 tablespoons plus 2 teaspoons butter, at room temperature

8 slices sourdough or other rustic white bread, sliced from a dense bakery loaf

8 ounces sharp cheddar or pepper Jack cheese, sliced

1 recipe *Rajas* (page 75)

—

4 panini

SHORT ON TIME? To save on prep time in the morning, grill the steak and *rajas* the night before. Quicker yet, just slice up any leftover steak you have on hand.

STEAK: Heat the panini press to high heat. If your panini press comes with a removable drip tray, make sure it is in place (see page 11).

Season both sides of the steak with salt, garlic powder, cumin, and pepper. Grill the steak, with the lid closed, to your desired doneness, 5 to 7 minutes for medium (137°F).

Transfer the steak to a cutting board and let it rest for 10 minutes before slicing it very thinly across the grain. Meanwhile, unplug the grill and, while it's still hot, carefully scrape down the grates with a grill scraper to remove any stuck-on bits of meat. Allow the grill to cool and clean the grates.

OMELETS: One at a time, prepare the omelets. Melt ½ teaspoon of the butter in a small nonstick skillet over medium-low heat. Beat 1 egg very well in a small bowl, season it with salt and pepper, and pour it into the skillet. Once the egg has set slightly, pull in the sides with a rubber spatula to allow the runny egg to flow to the edges of the pan. When the egg is nearly set, carefully lift up one edge with the rubber spatula and fold it in half. Transfer the omelet to a plate and tent it with foil to keep it warm while you prepare the other three omelets in the same manner.

PANINI: Reheat the panini press to medium-high heat.

(continued on next page)

FOR EACH SANDWICH: Spread butter on two slices of bread to flavor the outside of the sandwich. Flip over one slice of bread and layer on cheese, steak, an omelet, *rajas*, and more cheese. Close the sandwich with the other slice of bread, buttered side up.

Grill two panini at a time, with the lid closed, until the cheese is melted and the bread is toasted, 4 to 5 minutes.

Rajas

Even if you haven't heard the term *rajas* (pronounced RAH-has), chances are you've tasted them. They're simply bold-flavored strips of roasted chiles and onions, such as you might find served with fajitas. I grill them easily on the panini press, using mild poblano peppers, for use in all kinds of recipes—from sandwiches to tacos to pizzas.

1 poblano pepper (see Note)

1 red bell pepper

2 teaspoons vegetable oil

1 small white onion, sliced into ½-inch-thick rounds (rings intact)

—

About 2 cups

NOTE:

Some grocery stores may label poblano peppers as "pasilla" peppers, which is a technically incorrect (but common) reference to the green pepper in its fresh state.

Heat the panini press to medium-high heat.

Slice off the tops and bottoms of both peppers. Slice the poblano lengthwise down one side, spread it out flat, and remove the seeds. Cut the red bell pepper into three or four flat sections. Remove the seeds and trim any white ribs.

Lay the peppers, skin sides up, on the grill and close the lid. Grill the peppers until they're charred and blistered, 5 to 7 minutes. Transfer the peppers to a paper bag, close the bag, and let the peppers steam for 20 minutes to release their skins. One at a time, remove the peppers from the paper bag, peel off the skins (if they don't come off easily, try scraping them off with a paring knife), and slice the peppers lengthwise into strips. Transfer to a medium-size bowl.

While the peppers are steaming, drizzle both sides of the onion rounds with oil and grill them, with the lid closed, until they're tender and grill marks appear, 4 to 6 minutes. Separate the onions into rings and toss them with the peppers.

Use the *rajas* right away or refrigerate them, covered, for up to 3 days.

Marinated Lamb Chops

What do you mean he don't eat no meat?!" Aunt Voula reacts in disbelief to Toula's vegetarian fiancé in My Big Fat Greek Wedding. Everyone around them stops their conversations and stares. "That's okay. That's okay. I make lamb!"

Thanks to that hilarious movie I can't help but think to myself "I make lamb" whenever I'm getting ready to grill these chops. Not only are they an incredibly easy weeknight main dish—after marinating in the refrigerator overnight they grill in less than 20 minutes—but the juicy, flavorful meat (sorry, Aunt Voula!) is perfect for sandwiches. Use any leftovers for Marinated Lamb Shawarma (page 77).

¼ cup extra-virgin olive oil

¼ cup balsamic vinegar

2 teaspoons dried rosemary

2 garlic cloves, minced

1 teaspoon Dijon mustard

½ teaspoon freshly ground black pepper

2 pounds boneless lamb shoulder chops, about 1 inch thick (see Note)

½ teaspoon coarse salt

—

4 servings

NOTE:

Shoulder chops are usually sold boneless, but if you can find only bone-in chops, buy slightly more than 2 pounds. Bone-in chops may take a little longer to cook—be sure to check the temperature with a meat thermometer.

In a small bowl, whisk together the olive oil, balsamic vinegar, rosemary, garlic, mustard, and black pepper. Pour the marinade into a large zipper-top plastic bag. Add the lamb chops and gently massage the marinade into the meat. Seal the bag and marinate the lamb in the refrigerator for at least 4 hours, and preferably overnight.

Heat the panini press to high heat. If your panini press comes with a removable drip tray, make sure it is in place (see page 11).

Remove the lamb from the marinade (discard the remaining marinade) and pat it dry with paper towels. Season the lamb chops on both sides with salt. Working in batches, grill the lamb, with the lid closed, until it's cooked to an internal temperature of 145°F, 6 to 8 minutes. Allow the lamb to rest for 10 minutes on a cutting board before slicing it thinly across the grain.

Marinated Lamb Shawarma

Whenever I see a guy standing in a Middle Eastern food stand or restaurant expertly shaving thin strips of the most flavorful slow-roasted meat imaginable from a vertical spit, I find it nearly impossible to resist placing an order. Shawarma is the name not only of this incredible style of meat preparation, but also of the sandwiches made from this meat. Until I'm able to get one of those rotisseries installed in my house, I will settle for the next best way to make shawarma at home—with marinated lamb chops grilled on my panini press.

4 pita breads

4 red leaf lettuce leaves

2 medium-size ripe tomatoes, thinly sliced

½ cucumber, peeled and thinly sliced

¼ medium-size red onion, thinly sliced

1 recipe Marinated Lamb Chops (page 76)

1 recipe Lemon-Dill Yogurt Sauce (page 107)

—
4 shawarmas

FOR EACH SHAWARMA: If your pitas are dry, heat them for a few seconds in the microwave so they'll fold more easily without breaking. Lay a lettuce leaf on top of one of the pitas. Top it with tomatoes, cucumbers, onions, and lamb. Add a few spoonfuls of the yogurt sauce on top. Carefully fold the pita in half and enjoy.

CHAPTER 5

Gifts From the Sea

Seafood on the Panini Press

Smoked Salmon and Avocado Panini

If you enjoy smoked salmon with cream cheese, you've got to try it with avocado. Pureed avocado is just as creamy as cream cheese—even smoother, perhaps—and a squeeze of lemon juice gives it a nice tang (and salmon, as we know, tastes great with lemon). For these sandwiches, my idea of deluxe smoked salmon panini, I slather both cream cheese and my avocado spread on the bread and pile on beautiful smoked salmon, dill, tomatoes, and red onions.

4 tablespoons (½ stick) butter, at room temperature

8 slices pumpernickel bread, sliced from a dense bakery loaf

½ cup cream cheese, at room temperature

4 tablespoons Avocado Spread (recipe follows)

4 ounces smoked salmon

2 teaspoons chopped fresh dill

2 plum tomatoes (such as Roma), thinly sliced and seeded

½ small red onion, sliced

—

4 panini

Heat the panini press to medium-high heat.

FOR EACH SANDWICH: Spread butter on two slices of bread to flavor the outside of the sandwich. Flip over both slices of bread. Spread 2 tablespoons cream cheese on the other side of one slice and 1 tablespoon avocado spread on the other slice. Top the cream cheese with smoked salmon, dill, tomatoes, and red onion. Close the sandwich with the other slice of bread, buttered side up.

Grill two panini at a time, with the lid closed, until the bread is toasted, 3 to 4 minutes.

Avocado Spread

Avocado has a creamy texture like mayonnaise, but it's lower in overall fat and calories and high in nutrients like potassium and monounsaturated fats (which can help reduce your bad cholesterol and lower your risk of heart disease and stroke). When I'm looking for a creamy condiment that's lighter than mayonnaise and doesn't sacrifice an ounce of flavor, I puree avocado with lemon juice to make a smooth spread. Beyond panini, try this spread on top of salmon or other fish, as a dip for vegetables, or to cool a spicy gazpacho.

1 medium-size ripe avocado, pitted and peeled

1 tablespoon freshly squeezed lemon juice

¼ teaspoon coarse salt

⅛ teaspoon cayenne pepper

—
About ½ cup

In a small food processor or blender, puree the avocado, lemon juice, salt, and cayenne until it's smooth and creamy. Give the mixture a taste and season with more salt or lemon juice as needed. This spread is best if used the day it's made.

Grilled Shrimp Tostadas with Mashed Black Beans and Avocado Salsa Fresca

You can grill half a pound of shrimp on the panini press in about 2 minutes. That is reason enough to have panini-grilled shrimp in your regular weeknight dinner rotation, don't you think?

For these tostadas I first let the shrimp bathe in a chili-lime marinade before they hit the grill. Also grilled on the panini press: the tostada shells. You just brush a little oil on regular tortillas and after a minute or so on the grill they're toasty, crisp, and ready for toppings. Black beans mashed with garlic (a terrific technique I learned from a Rick Bayless recipe) and sprinkled with *queso fresco* make a flavorful base to hold the shrimp on the tostada, and an avocado salsa fresca brings a punch of bright, Southwestern flavor to the dish.

SHRIMP

2 tablespoons vegetable oil

1 teaspoon freshly squeezed lime juice

1 teaspoon chili powder

¼ teaspoon ground cumin

¼ teaspoon coarse salt

1 pound raw large shrimp, peeled and deveined

MASHED BLACK BEANS

2 tablespoons vegetable oil

3 garlic cloves, minced

1 (15-ounce) can black beans, rinsed and drained

1 to 2 tablespoons water

Coarse salt

TOSTADAS

1 tablespoon vegetable oil

4 (8-inch) flour tortillas

Coarse salt

4 ounces (about 1 cup) crumbled queso fresco or shredded Monterey Jack

1 cup Avocado Salsa Fresca (page 84)

—

4 tostadas

SHRIMP: In a medium-size bowl, stir together the vegetable oil, lime juice, chili powder, cumin, and salt. Add the shrimp and toss to coat them in the marinade. Cover the bowl and let the shrimp marinate in the refrigerator while you prepare the rest of the dish. (Note: The citric acid in the lime juice can start to "cook" the shrimp after a while, so I don't recommend marinating the shrimp for longer than 30 minutes.)

MASHED BLACK BEANS: Heat the vegetable oil in a large skillet over medium heat. Add the garlic and stir it in the oil until it's fragrant and just beginning to brown, about 1 minute. Add the black beans. Give the beans a rough mash with a potato masher (they should still be a bit chunky) and cook them for another minute or two until they're heated through. Take the pan off the heat and stir in 1 to 2 tablespoons of water, until the beans are spreadable. Season the beans with coarse salt to taste and partially cover the pan to keep them warm.

TOSTADAS: Heat the panini press to medium-high heat.

Lightly brush a tortilla with vegetable oil and transfer it to the grill. Sprinkle the tortilla with a little salt and close the lid. Grill the tortilla until it's crisped and golden grill marks appear, 1 to 2 minutes. Repeat with the rest of the tortillas. Keep the grill heated.

(continued)

Remove the shrimp from the marinade (discard the remaining marinade) and put half of them on the grill. Close the lid and grill the shrimp until they're cooked through and opaque, about 2 minutes. Repeat with the remaining shrimp.

Spread some mashed black beans over each grilled tortilla (if the beans have cooled off too much to be spreadable, put them back on the stove over low heat for a few minutes and stir in water, 1 teaspoon at a time). Top them with *queso fresco*, grilled shrimp, and avocado salsa fresca and serve.

Avocado Salsa Fresca

Mix up this fresh and easy avocado salsa and set it in the refrigerator; by the time you're done preparing the tostadas, the flavors will have had a chance to blend together just right. Scoop up any leftover salsa with tortilla chips or use it to top tacos, fish, or crostini.

1 medium-size ripe avocado, pitted, peeled, and diced

2 medium-size ripe tomatoes, diced

3 tablespoons chopped red onion

½ jalapeño pepper, seeded and finely chopped

2 tablespoons chopped fresh cilantro

1 tablespoon freshly squeezed lime juice

¼ teaspoon coarse salt

—
About 2½ cups

Toss all of the ingredients together in a medium-size bowl. Cover the bowl and refrigerate for 30 minutes to allow the flavors to combine. The salsa is best the day it's made, but it will stay fresh in the refrigerator for up to 2 days.

Grilled Salmon Packets with Pesto and Tomatoes

Grilling food in a foil or parchment packet is an easy, efficient way to steam a number of items all at once, allow their flavors to meld, and retain the food's moisture. Here, "packet grilling" produces a moist and flavorful salmon with basil pesto and fresh tomatoes. This recipe is adapted from one my friend Kalyn Denny created on her blog, Kalynskitchen.com. The entire dish takes just 20 minutes to prepare and, since you cook it inside the packet, there's nearly no cleanup!

2 teaspoons extra-virgin olive oil

1 (1-pound) skin-on center-cut salmon fillet

2 to 3 tablespoons pesto, purchased or homemade (page 45)

1 medium-size tomato, sliced about ¼ inch thick

—
2 to 3 servings

Heat the panini press to high heat.

Drizzle olive oil in the center of a piece of foil large enough to wrap the salmon with some overlapping. Lay the salmon on top of the oil. Spread pesto all over the top of the salmon. Arrange the sliced tomatoes over the pesto so that they cover the top of the salmon.

Wrap the salmon securely in the foil, doubling over the seam and ends several times. Take care to create a flat seam on top so that the grill lid can heat the surface evenly. Place the salmon packet on the grill. Close the lid so that the upper plate makes contact with the packet without pressing it. Grill for 10 minutes.

Remove the salmon from the grill and let it sit for 2 to 3 minutes before carefully opening the packet. Serve immediately.

Grilled Salmon with Old Bay Aioli

My first real taste of Old Bay seasoning, the Baltimore specialty, actually wasn't on crab or any other seafood. It was on French fries I bought on the boardwalk in Bethany Beach, Delaware, a few years ago on a family vacation. Talk about flavor! There is definitely something about the combination of salt, a little heat, and some subtle sweetness that makes you want to shake this stuff on just about everything. The spice blend dates back to the 1940s, but it's as popular as ever today, especially in the Mid-Atlantic.

A spoonful of Old Bay in the aioli that dresses this grilled salmon adds wonderful complexity to its flavor. The salmon itself is as simple as can be—just seasoned with salt and pepper and grilled for 7 minutes—so even on a busy weeknight, you'll have time to whip up this fabulous sauce and enjoy a quick yet sophisticated meal.

2 tablespoons extra-virgin olive oil

Coarse salt and freshly ground black pepper

1 (1-pound) skin-on center-cut salmon fillet, cut into 4 portions

1 recipe Old Bay Aioli (recipe follows)

—

4 servings

Heat the panini press to medium-high heat. If your panini press comes with a removable drip tray, make sure it is in place (see page 11).

Pour the olive oil into a shallow bowl or glass pie plate. Add the salmon to the dish and turn each piece to coat with olive oil. Season the salmon with salt and pepper.

Place the salmon on the grill, skin side down, and close the lid so that the upper plate makes contact with the salmon without pressing it. Grill until the salmon is cooked through and opaque, 6 to 7 minutes, depending on the thickness of the fish.

Serve the salmon with the Old Bay Aioli.

Old Bay Aioli

I can't promise that you won't start hunting around your fridge and pantry for other items to dunk into this fantastic aioli. Seafood is the most natural pairing for Old Bay–seasoned condiments, but you might also serve this aioli along with crudités or French fries, or even on hamburgers.

1 large egg yolk

1½ teaspoons apple cider vinegar

1½ teaspoons freshly squeezed lemon juice

1 garlic clove, minced

1 anchovy fillet, minced

¾ cup vegetable oil

¼ cup extra-virgin olive oil

1 teaspoon Old Bay seasoning

—

About 1 cup

Roll up a kitchen towel and wrap it around the base of a medium-size bowl to keep it stable. Whisk together the egg yolk, vinegar, lemon juice, garlic, and anchovy until well combined.

Start adding the vegetable oil a few drops at a time while whisking vigorously. Continue whisking while gradually pouring in the remaining vegetable oil in a thin, thread-like stream. The mixture will slowly turn an opaque golden yellow. As you add more oil, the aioli will become thicker and creamy and take on a paler yellow color.

Whisk in the olive oil, also in a thin stream. Whisk in the Old Bay seasoning. Give the aioli a taste and add more lemon juice if it needs it. Cover the bowl and refrigerate the aioli until you're ready to use it, for up to 4 days.

Seared Ahi and Avocado Salad

One of my best friends doesn't consider herself to be much of a cook, but she knows good, healthy food when she eats it. The queen of our local takeout scene, she is fully prepared for any last-minute ordering, with all of the restaurants programmed into her cell phone. A favorite order of hers is a seared ahi salad that's been tossed in ginger vinaigrette with goodies like avocado, edamame, roasted red bell peppers, and greens. I ventured to make my own version at home—searing the ahi to perfection on the panini press for a mere 90 seconds—and was won over by this fabulous Cal-Asian salad combination as well.

TUNA

1 tablespoon extra-virgin olive oil

1 (1-pound) sashimi-grade ahi tuna steak, about 1 inch thick

Coarse salt and freshly ground black pepper

SALAD

1 head butter lettuce, torn into large pieces

¼ red onion, thinly sliced

½ cup sliced roasted red bell peppers

½ cup shelled cooked edamame, thawed if frozen

1 recipe Ginger Vinaigrette (recipe follows)

1 medium-size ripe avocado, pitted, peeled, and sliced

—

4 servings

TUNA: Heat the panini press to high heat. If your panini press comes with a removable drip tray, make sure it is in place (see page 11).

Brush the olive oil over both sides of the tuna and season the tuna with salt and pepper.

Grill the tuna, with the lid closed, until it's seared on the outside but still bright red on the inside, about 90 seconds. Transfer the fish to a cutting board and slice it thinly across the grain.

SALAD: Toss the lettuce, onion, peppers, edamame, and 2 tablespoons of the ginger vinaigrette together in a large bowl.

Divide the salad among four plates. Arrange slices of tuna and avocado on top of each salad and drizzle more ginger vinaigrette over the top (you probably will have extra dressing for later use).

Ginger Vinaigrette

When it comes to salad dressings, I'm a vinaigrette girl all the way. Once you've got the classic ratio down—3 parts oil, 1 part vinegar or other acid—you can customize vinaigrettes to fit any flavor profile. For Asian-inspired salads, a ginger-based dressing is a perfect complement.

1 tablespoon reduced-sodium soy sauce

1 tablespoon freshly squeezed lemon juice

1 tablespoon plus 2 teaspoons rice wine vinegar

2 garlic cloves, minced

2 teaspoons grated fresh ginger

1 teaspoon honey

½ teaspoon Dijon mustard

½ teaspoon sugar

½ cup extra-virgin olive oil

Freshly ground black pepper

—
About ¾ cup

In a small bowl, whisk together the soy sauce, lemon juice, vinegar, garlic, ginger, honey, mustard, and sugar. Gradually whisk in the olive oil. Season the vinaigrette with black pepper to taste. Store any leftovers in an airtight container in the refrigerator for up to 4 days.

Grilled Fish Tacos

When out-of-town friends come to visit us in San Diego, there's one local delicacy that's always high on their list to try: fish tacos. They first became popular down in Baja California and, thankfully, found their way north of the border. When you're used to having mainly chicken or steak in your tortilla, fish tacos may sound a little odd, but trust me—they're San Diego's most popular dish for good reason.

Grilling the fish on the panini press takes a matter of minutes and it comes out moist, flaky, and flavorful. I add some spicy chipotles to the traditional sour cream sauce to boost the overall flavor even further.

FISH

¼ cup vegetable oil

2 tablespoons freshly squeezed lime juice

2 teaspoons ancho chili powder

¼ teaspoon coarse salt

1 (1-pound) flaky white fish fillet, such as mahi mahi or halibut

ACCOMPANIMENTS

8 (8-inch) corn or flour tortillas, warmed

Shredded cabbage

Hot sauce or salsa

Sliced red onions

Sliced scallions

Chipotle Sour Cream (recipe follows)

Chopped fresh cilantro

Lime wedges

—
4 servings

FISH: Whisk together the oil, lime juice, ancho chile powder, and salt in a shallow glass dish. Add the fish and turn to coat it in the marinade. Cover the dish and let the fish marinate in the refrigerator for 20 minutes.

Heat the panini press to medium-high heat. If your panini press comes with a removable drip tray, make sure it is in place (see page 11).

Transfer the fish to the grill and close the lid so that the upper plate is resting on the fish without pressing it. Grill the fish until it's cooked through, 3 to 4 minutes. With a spatula, carefully transfer the fish to a plate.

Divide the fish among the tortillas (it should flake easily) and top each taco with cabbage, salsa, onions, scallions, and a dollop of chipotle sour cream. Garnish with a little chopped cilantro and serve with lime wedges.

Chipotle Sour Cream

Good things come to those who wait . . . but you won't have to wait long at all to enjoy this quick and easy sauce on top of your tacos, quesadillas, or any other dish that could use a spicy-yet-cool boost.

¼ cup sour cream

¼ cup mayonnaise

3 tablespoons freshly squeezed lime juice

1 chipotle in adobo sauce, minced

—

About ¾ cup

In a small bowl, whisk together the sour cream, mayonnaise, lime juice, and chipotle. Cover the bowl and refrigerate the mixture until you're ready to use it. It will stay fresh in the refrigerator for about 3 days.

CHAPTER 6

Nature's Bounty

Fruit, Vegetables, and Beans on the Panini Press

Heirloom Tomato Panini

I couldn't have imagined how such simple ingredients—and so few of them—could combine into such blissfully sweet, salty, briny bites. The beauty of this sandwich is in its simplicity. Take a few minutes to whip up your own olive oil mayonnaise—it's well worth it.

4 tablespoons (½ stick) butter, at room temperature

8 slices sourdough bread, sliced from a dense bakery loaf

4 tablespoons Olive Oil Mayonnaise (recipe follows) or purchased mayonnaise

2 medium-size ripe heirloom tomatoes, thickly sliced

Coarse salt and freshly ground black pepper

—

4 panini

Heat the panini press to high.

FOR EACH SANDWICH: Spread butter on two slices of bread to flavor the outside of the sandwich. Flip over both slices and spread 1 tablespoon mayonnaise on the other side of each. Layer enough tomato slices onto one slice of bread to cover it. Season the tomatoes with salt and pepper. Close the sandwich with the other slice of bread, buttered side up.

Place two panini on the grill and close the lid so that the lid is resting on the top of the sandwiches without pressing them. Grill the panini, two at a time, just until the bread is toasted, 1 to 2 minutes.

Olive Oil Mayonnaise

The approach below is delightfully inexact, drawn from Amy Finley's food memoir, *How to Eat a Small Country* (Clarkson Potter, 2011). In the book, the author learns an important lesson about cooking and about life: relax and let go.

1 egg yolk

A slosh of white wine vinegar

A sprinkle of salt

A spoonful of Dijon mustard

1 cup extra-light olive oil

—

About 1 cup

Roll up a kitchen towel and wrap it around the base of a medium-size bowl to keep it stable. Whisk together the egg yolk, white wine vinegar, salt, and Dijon mustard until well combined. Continue whisking briskly while pouring the olive oil slowly and steadily into the bowl, until the mayonnaise is emulsified, light, and fluffy.

Refrigerate any unused mayonnaise in a covered bowl. It's best to use it within 3 days.

Caprese Panini

When people get a new panini press and ask me which sandwich they should grill first, I always suggest the classic combination of tomato, basil, and mozzarella. Based on the Italian insalata caprese, it couldn't be simpler, and meat lovers and vegetarians alike love it. For the best results, be sure to use really sweet, ripe summer tomatoes.

1 French baguette, cut into 4 portions, or 4 mini baguettes

½ cup pesto, purchased or homemade (page 45)

4 ounces fresh mozzarella cheese, sliced

2 medium-size ripe tomatoes, sliced

8 fresh basil leaves

—

4 panini

Heat the panini press to medium-high heat.

FOR EACH SANDWICH: Slice off the domed top of a baguette portion to create a flat grilling surface. Split the baguette to create top and bottom halves. Spread a layer of pesto inside each baguette half. On the bottom half layer some mozzarella, tomatoes, basil, and more mozzarella. Close the sandwich with the top baguette half.

Grill two panini at a time, with the lid closed, until the cheese is melted and the bread is toasted, 5 to 6 minutes.

Marinated Portobello Mushroom Panini

A portobello mushroom is simply a brown cremini mushroom that's matured and grown a large cap. Thick and meaty, these large caps can absorb a tremendous amount of flavor from a marinade.

1 French baguette, cut into 4 portions, or 4 mini baguettes

½ cup pesto, purchased or homemade (page 45)

4 ounces Manchego cheese, sliced

4 Marinated Portobello Mushrooms (recipe follows)

8 oil-packed sun-dried tomatoes, thinly sliced

4 fresh basil leaves, roughly torn

—

4 panini

Heat the panini press to medium-high heat.

FOR EACH SANDWICH: Slice off the domed top of a baguette portion to create a flat grilling surface. Split the baguette. Spread a thin layer of pesto inside each baguette half. On the lower half, layer cheese, a mushroom cap, sun-dried tomatoes, basil, and more cheese. Close the sandwich.

Grill two panini at a time, with the lid closed, until the cheese is melted and the baguettes are toasted, 7 to 9 minutes.

MAKE IT AHEAD: You can marinate and grill your mushrooms ahead of time—they'll keep for 3 to 5 days in a covered container in the refrigerator.

Marinated Portobello Mushrooms

Portobello mushroom caps can soak up marinade like a sponge and grill in just minutes on the panini press. This is great news for vegetarians and omnivores alike.

4 portobello mushrooms

¼ cup extra-virgin olive oil

¼ cup balsamic vinegar

2 garlic cloves, minced

1 teaspoon dried thyme

1 teaspoon Dijon mustard

½ teaspoon coarse salt

¼ teaspoon freshly ground black pepper

—

4 servings

Wipe any dirt from the mushroom caps with a damp paper towel. Pop out the stems and scoop out the gills with a spoon; discard the stems and gills.

Combine the olive oil, vinegar, garlic, thyme, mustard, salt, and pepper in a shallow bowl. Add the mushroom caps and roll them around in the marinade a bit to coat them turning them occasionally, for 30 minutes.

Heat the panini press to medium-high heat. If your panini press comes with a removable drip tray, make sure it is in place (see page 11).

Remove the mushrooms from the marinade (discard the remaining marinade), transfer them to the grill, and close the lid. Grill the mushrooms until they're tender and dark grill marks appear, about 5 minutes.

Portobello Patty Melt Panini

My sister Julie told me about a dish she makes of portobello mushrooms topped with Asiago cheese and leeks and then slipped under the broiler. That sounded like a great panini idea to me, so I gave it a try. A few little tweaks and—voilà!—these panini were born. In place of leeks, I use my perennial favorite, sweet caramelized onions, and I've added fresh baby arugula. With all of the bright flavors in here, this just might be my very favorite meatless sandwich.

1 ciabatta loaf, cut into 4 portions, or 4 ciabatta rolls

8 ounces Asiago cheese, sliced

1 cup Caramelized Onions (page 19)

4 Marinated Portobello Mushrooms (page 96)

1 cup baby arugula

—

4 panini

Heat the panini press to medium-high heat.

FOR EACH SANDWICH: Split a ciabatta portion to create top and bottom halves. On the bottom half layer cheese, caramelized onions, a mushroom cap (cut in half, if necessary, to fit on the bread), arugula, and more cheese. Close the sandwich with the top ciabatta half.

Grill two panini at a time, with the lid closed, until the cheese is melted and the ciabatta is toasted, 8 to 10 minutes.

Grilled Herbed Vegetables

When I grill vegetables I like to make a large batch and then I use them for days, as a side dish, in sandwiches and salads, over pasta—you name it. They'll stay fresh for several days in the refrigerator. These fresh eggplants, zucchini, bell peppers, and onions get a good drenching in balsamic vinegar, olive oil, and herbs for robust Mediterranean flavor.

¼ cup extra-virgin olive oil

2 tablespoons balsamic vinegar

2 tablespoons dried parsley

2 tablespoons dried basil

1 tablespoon dried marjoram

1 teaspoon coarse salt

½ teaspoon freshly ground black pepper

6 garlic cloves, minced

2 Japanese eggplants, sliced lengthwise into ¼-inch-thick strips

2 small zucchini, sliced lengthwise into ¼-inch-thick strips

1 red bell pepper, cored, seeded, and sliced into ½-inch-thick strips

1 yellow bell pepper, cored, seeded, and sliced into ½-inch-thick strips

1 small red onion

—

6 to 8 servings

In a large zipper-top plastic bag, combine the olive oil, vinegar, parsley, basil, marjoram, salt, pepper, and garlic. Place the eggplants, zucchini, and bell peppers in the bag (reserve the onion). Seal the bag, roll the vegetables around in the marinade to coat them, and let the vegetables marinate for 1 to 2 hours in the refrigerator.

Heat the panini press to medium-high heat. If your panini press comes with a removable drip tray, make sure it is in place (see page 11).

Remove the vegetables from the marinade and reserve 1 tablespoon of the marinade. Grill the vegetables in batches of the same type of vegetable (all of the eggplant together, all of the zucchini together, etc.), with the lid closed, until they are tender and grill marks appear, 4 to 6 minutes, depending on the type of vegetable. Arrange the vegetables on a serving platter as they come off the grill. Slice the onion into ¼-inch-thick rounds. Drizzle the reserved marinade over the onions and grill them, with the lid closed, until they are tender and grill marks appear, 4 to 6 minutes. Serve the vegetables immediately or at room temperature.

Grilled Cheese Panzanella Salad

Panzanella is a true summertime treat. Chunks of day-old bread tossed with just-off-the-vine tomatoes, fresh basil, olive oil, and vinegar make up this traditional Italian salad. The dressing and juices from the tomatoes soak in and flavor the dry bread, which is where the real magic happens.

I had an idea one day . . . why not turn those chunks of stale bread into mini grilled cheese sandwiches? Traditionally, there's no cheese in panzanella, but there's no denying that mozzarella pairs perfectly with tomatoes and basil. I say food is food, so let's have fun with it. And nothing says fun, at least in the sandwich world, like teeny-tiny grilled cheese sandwiches in a salad.

GRILLED CHEESE CROUTONS

4 slices day-old sourdough or other rustic white bread, sliced from a dense bakery loaf

2 ounces (about ½ cup) shredded mozzarella or other semi-firm cheese

SALAD

4 medium-size ripe tomatoes, cut into bite-size chunks

½ small red onion, thinly sliced

¼ cup torn fresh basil leaves

1 recipe White Balsamic Vinaigrette (page 37)

—
About 4 servings

GRILLED CHEESE CROUTONS: Heat the panini press to medium-high heat.

Place half the cheese on each of two slices of bread. Close each sandwich with a second slice of bread.

Grill both panini, with the lid closed, until the cheese is melted and the bread is toasted, 3 to 4 minutes. Transfer the panini to a cutting board. Trim the crusts from the panini and cut each sandwich into 1-inch squares.

SALAD: Place the tomatoes, sliced onions, torn basil, and grilled cheese croutons in a large salad bowl.

Toss the salad with enough of the dressing to moisten the croutons without drenching them. Allow the flavors to meld at room temperature for 30 minutes before serving the salad.

Egg White Omelet Panino with Spinach, Feta, and Sun-Dried Tomatoes

I was waiting for a flight at the Atlanta airport when I noticed a young woman in her 20s who had just exited a plane. From afar, she gazed up at the familiar green-and-white logo of that ubiquitous Seattle-based coffee giant, stretched out her arms, and screamed, "Sanctuary!" I don't know where she'd been traveling or how long she'd been away, but I can relate to feeling a little perk in my mood when a branch of this particular establishment appears in my path just when I need it.

Beyond the coffee—mostly decaf for me these days—I've become a fan of the food at this coffee chain. One item in particular, a spinach and feta breakfast wrap made with egg whites, is so flavorful and satisfying that I easily forget that it's classed as a healthier option. The egg whites pack a lot of protein, feta is naturally low in fat, and the green, leafy spinach is loaded with nutrients. One day I ventured to make my own version of this fabulous wrap and it came together in a snap.

3 large egg whites

Coarse salt and freshly ground black pepper

2 slices sourdough or other rustic white bread, sliced from a dense bakery loaf

¼ cup loosely packed baby spinach

3 oil-packed sun-dried tomatoes, thinly sliced

1 ounce crumbled feta cheese

—

1 panino (see Note)

NOTE:

You can easily scale up this recipe to make more servings; just be sure to cook the egg white omelets one at a time.

Spray a little nonstick cooking spray in a small skillet and heat it over medium-high heat.

Meanwhile, in a large bowl, whisk the egg whites until they're frothy. Season them with salt and pepper. Pour the egg whites into the skillet and let them cook until they're set on the bottom, about 1 minute. With a spatula, carefully lift up one side and fold it over, creating a half-moon shape. Continue cooking the omelet, flipping after another minute or so, until it's cooked through and set. Slide the omelet onto a plate and tent it with foil to keep it warm while you assemble the sandwich.

Heat the panini press to medium-high heat.

Create a little bed of baby spinach on one slice of bread and lay your egg white omelet on top of it. Arrange the sun-dried tomato slices on the omelet and sprinkle the feta on top. Close the sandwich with the other slice of bread.

Grill the sandwich, with the lid closed, until the cheese is softened and the bread is toasted, 4 to 5 minutes.

PANINI VS. PANINIS VS. PANINO

In America it's common to hear people refer to a single grilled sandwich as "a panini" and multiple sandwiches as "paninis." These words have become part of the popular lexicon, but they drive linguistic purists absolutely crazy.

Technically speaking, there is no such word as "paninis." The word "panini" is already in the plural form—it's Italian for "sandwiches." Saying "paninis" is like saying "sandwicheses," And saying "a panini" is like saying "a sandwiches." Doesn't sound quite right, does it?

So what's the correct word to refer to just one grilled sandwich? The singular form of the word "panini" is "panino." One panino . . . two panini.

You're probably thinking to yourself, "Whoever heard of a panino?" Well, you're right, it's not a commonly used word here in the United States. Chances are you might be met with blank stares if you try to use it. To me, it's important to respect the integrity of a language, but it's also important to communicate and be understood. At the end of the day, as long as the sandwich tastes great, it doesn't matter to me what you call it!

Grilled Tomato Soup with Herbed Grilled Cheese Croutons

I knew I had a hit with this grilled tomato soup when I brought it to one of our local San Diego food blogger potlucks and, one by one, each person glanced up from her bowl and asked, "Who made the soup? I love it!" It intrigued them to learn that I'd actually grilled the tomatoes and onions for the soup on the panini press. It's another example of how you can use the panini press as a prep tool for all kinds of dishes.

2 pounds plum tomatoes (such as Roma), halved lengthwise

1 to 2 cups low-sodium vegetable broth

2 tablespoons extra-virgin olive oil

Coarse salt and freshly ground black pepper

1 medium-size yellow onion, sliced into ½-inch-thick rounds (rings intact)

1 red bell pepper, cored, seeded, and chopped

3 garlic cloves, minced

⅛ teaspoon red pepper flakes

1 teaspoon sugar

2 tablespoons chopped fresh parsley

1 sprig fresh thyme

1 recipe Herbed Grilled Cheese Croutons (page 104)

—

4 servings

Heat the panini press to high heat. If your panini press comes with a removable drip tray, make sure it is in place (see page 11).

Place a strainer over a 2-cup liquid measuring cup. Scoop out the pulp and seeds from the tomato halves into the strainer and press down with a spoon to collect all of the tomato juice. Add enough vegetable broth to the measuring cup to bring the total amount of liquid to 2 cups. Set aside.

Drizzle the cut sides of the tomato halves with 1½ teaspoons of the olive oil and season with salt and pepper. In batches, place the tomatoes, cut sides down, on the grill. Close the lid, making light contact with the tomatoes without pressing them. Grill the tomatoes until they are soft and the outer skins are wrinkly, 8 to 10 minutes.

Drizzle the onion rounds with another 1½ teaspoons of the olive oil and season with salt and pepper. Place the onions on the grill. Close the lid, making light contact with the onions without pressing them. Grill the onions until they are tender and grill marks appear, 4 to 6 minutes.

Transfer the onions to a cutting board, let them cool a bit, and give them a rough chop.

Heat the remaining 1 tablespoon olive oil in a Dutch oven or large saucepan over medium heat. Add the red bell pepper and cook, stirring often, until it begins to soften, 4 to 5 minutes. Add the garlic and red pepper flakes and cook until fragrant, about 1 minute more. Stir in the grilled tomatoes, grilled onions, sugar, parsley, thyme sprig, and vegetable stock mixture.

(continued)

Bring the soup to a boil, reduce the heat, and simmer, uncovered, for 40 minutes. Remove the thyme sprig.

Puree the soup either with an immersion blender or in batches in a blender or food processor. Season with salt and pepper to taste.

Serve the soup hot with the croutons.

Herbed Grilled Cheese Croutons

I think these grilled cheese croutons are so cute. Obviously, they're nothing more than grilled cheese sandwiches that have been cut into small squares. I use fresh herb butter on the outside to make them extra-crisp and savory. We all love to eat grilled cheese sandwiches with tomato soup . . . so why not put them in the soup? Add these croutons to any soup, chili, or stew that you might otherwise pair with a grilled cheese sandwich. You could also use them to top salads, such as the Grilled Cheese Panzanella Salad (page 99).

2 tablespoons butter, at room temperature

1 teaspoon chopped fresh basil

½ teaspoon chopped fresh chives

½ teaspoon chopped fresh thyme

4 slices sourdough bread, sliced from a dense bakery loaf

4 ounces semi-firm cheese such as cheddar, Colby, or Monterey Jack, sliced

—

4 servings

Mix the butter and herbs in a small bowl.

Spread herb butter on one side of each slice of bread. Turn over two of the bread slices and top them with cheese. Close each sandwich with the remaining slices of bread, buttered sides up. Grill the panini until the cheese is melted and the bread is toasted, 3 to 4 minutes. Transfer the panini to a cutting board. Trim the crusts from the panini and cut each sandwich into 1-inch squares.

Grilled Tofu and Bok Choy Bowl

I love a good weeknight recipe that requires less than 10 minutes of active cooking time. Let the tofu drain its water and soak in the savory Asian-style marinade while you handle the things that need handling around your house. Then toss the tofu and baby bok choy on the panini press for just minutes to get a nice sear and serve it all over steamed rice. Fast, healthy, delicious—you'll keep coming back to this one.

1 (14-ounce) package extra-firm tofu

3 tablespoons reduced-sodium soy sauce

1 tablespoon vegetable oil

2 teaspoons rice vinegar

1 teaspoon toasted sesame oil

1½ teaspoons honey

1 teaspoon grated fresh ginger

1 small garlic clove, minced

¼ teaspoon red pepper flakes

2 baby bok choy, halved lengthwise

2 cups steamed brown or white rice, for serving

Chopped scallions and toasted sesame seeds, for garnish

—
4 servings

Stack a few paper towels on a cutting board. Drain the water from the tofu package. Slice the tofu in half horizontally into two slabs, each about ¾ inch thick, and then cut each slab into 4 crosswise sections for a total of 8 pieces. Lay the tofu pieces side by side on the paper towels. Cover the tofu with more paper towels and set a heavy, flat object, like a baking sheet with a heavy skillet on it, on top to press the water out of the tofu. Press for 30 to 60 minutes.

While the tofu is being pressed, get the marinade ready. Whisk together the soy sauce, vegetable oil, vinegar, sesame oil, honey, ginger, garlic, and red pepper flakes in a glass pie plate. Lay the tofu pieces in the marinade and let them soak for 8 minutes. Flip them over and soak them for another 8 minutes.

Heat the panini press to high heat.

Transfer the tofu to the grill, reserving the remaining marinade. Close the lid and grill the tofu until grill marks appear, 2 to 3 minutes. Transfer the grilled tofu to a plate.

Pat the bok choy dry and place it, cut sides down, on the grill. Grill the bok choy until it's tender and grill marks appear, 2 to 3 minutes.

Meanwhile, pour the reserved marinade into a small saucepan and bring it to a boil. Simmer it for 2 minutes, then remove the pan from the heat.

Transfer the bok choy to a cutting board and slice it crosswise into bite-sized pieces.

Divide the rice among four bowls. Top the rice with tofu and bok choy and drizzle on the simmered marinade. Garnish with chopped scallions and toasted sesame seeds.

Spinach-Feta Quinoa Cakes with Lemon-Dill Yogurt Sauce

We're meat-eaters in our house, without a doubt. But we don't mind a good veggie burger every now and then either—especially if it's got lots of great flavor. I like to make mine with quinoa (pronounced KEEN-wa). Even though many people consider quinoa to be a grain, it's actually a closer relative to beets, spinach, and Swiss chard. With its high protein content, it earns the status of a "superfood." And it happens to be very easy and versatile to cook with—even on the panini press.

1 tablespoon extra-virgin olive oil

½ cup finely chopped onion

2 garlic cloves, finely chopped

5 ounces baby spinach, chopped

2 large eggs, beaten

1¼ cups cooked quinoa

2 ounces crumbled feta cheese

1 tablespoon chopped fresh dill

¼ teaspoon grated lemon zest

¼ teaspoon freshly ground black pepper

½ cup bread crumbs

1 recipe Lemon-Dill Yogurt Sauce (recipe follows)

—

4 servings (8 to 10 patties)

These grilled quinoa cakes take on the zesty flavors of a classic Greek spanakopita. Spoon a little lemon-dill yogurt sauce over the top for a light, healthy lunch.

Heat the olive oil in a large skillet over medium heat. Add the onion and garlic and cook, stirring often, until softened, about 4 minutes. Add the spinach and cook, stirring often, until wilted, about 3 minutes. Transfer the mixture to a medium-size bowl.

Add the eggs, quinoa, feta, dill, lemon zest, and black pepper and mix well. Mix in the bread crumbs and let the mixture sit for a few minutes to allow the bread crumbs to absorb some of the moisture.

Heat the panini press to medium-high heat.

Form quinoa patties about 2½ inches in diameter and ½ inch thick. Place the patties on the grill, in batches if necessary, and close the lid. Grill the patties until they're cooked through and browned on the outside, 4 to 5 minutes. Serve warm with lemon-dill yogurt sauce.

Lemon-Dill Yogurt Sauce

This cool, creamy sauce brightens up all kinds of dishes, from salmon to falafel to raw vegetables. It tastes even better once the flavors have had a chance to meld, so make it at least 30 minutes before you need it, if possible.

½ cup plain Greek yogurt, reduced fat or whole

2 tablespoons finely chopped scallions

2 teaspoons freshly squeezed lemon juice

2 teaspoons chopped fresh dill

Coarse salt and freshly ground black pepper

—
About ½ cup

Whisk together the yogurt, scallions, lemon juice, and dill in a small bowl. Season to taste with salt and pepper. Cover and refrigerate the sauce for at least 30 minutes to allow the flavors to meld.

Grilled Tomatillo Guacamole

I finally put my finger on the not-so-secret ingredient that makes my favorite restaurant guacamole, from El Nopalito in Encinitas, California, especially fresh-tasting: tomatillos. The tart, green cousins of tomatoes are a staple in Mexican cuisine. They're nearly camouflaged by the avocados in the guacamole, but you can taste their presence in that je ne sais quoi kind of way. To dial down the tartness a little and coax out the sweetness, I grill the tomatillos for just a few minutes on the panini press before mixing them into the dip.

2 tomatillos, husks removed

2 teaspoons extra-virgin olive oil

3 medium-size ripe avocados, pitted, peeled, and chopped

¼ cup chopped red onion

½ jalapeño pepper, seeded and finely chopped

2 tablespoons chopped fresh cilantro

1 tablespoon freshly squeezed lime juice

½ teaspoon ground cumin

½ teaspoon coarse salt

¼ teaspoon freshly ground black pepper

1 recipe Grilled Tortilla Chips (page 109)

—
8 to 10 servings

Heat the panini press to medium-high heat. If your panini press comes with a removable drip tray, make sure it is in place (see page 11).

Slice the tomatillos in half and drizzle olive oil on the cut sides. Place the tomatillos on the grill, cut sides down, and close the lid so that it's resting on the tomatillos without pressing them. Grill the tomatillos until they're softened and grill marks appear, 2 to 3 minutes.

Chop the tomatillos and place them in a large bowl. Add the avocados, onion, jalapeño, cilantro, lime juice, cumin, salt, and pepper to the bowl and mash it all together with a fork to a uniform but still chunky consistency.

Serve the guacamole with tortilla chips.

Grilled Tortilla Chips

After I grilled my first tortilla shells for Shrimp Tostadas (page 82) and felt their light, crisp crunch upon taking a bite, I realized I had the makings for some pretty easy tortilla chips as well. I brainstormed a bit and came up with three simple flavor combinations that would make these chips tasty for snacking on their own or as an elegant accompaniment for guacamole or cheeses: lemon–black pepper, chile-garlic, and coriander-lime.

2 tablespoons extra-virgin olive oil

⅛ teaspoon coarse salt

Additional seasonings (see below), optional

2 (8-inch) soft corn or flour tortillas

—

16 chips

Heat the panini press to high heat.

In a small bowl, combine the olive oil, salt, and additional seasonings, if desired.

Brush each tortilla generously on both sides with the seasoned oil. With a pizza cutter or a sharp knife, cut each tortilla into 8 triangles.

Grill the triangles, with the lid closed completely, until they're browned and crisped, about 90 seconds for flour tortillas or 2 minutes for corn tortillas. Serve them warm or at room temperature.

Flavor	Additional Seasonings	Recommended Pairings
Lemon–Black Pepper	½ teaspoon freshly grated lemon zest ⅛ teaspoon freshly ground black pepper	Hummus, white bean dip, smoked salmon, goat cheese
Chile-Garlic	½ teaspoon chili powder ¼ teaspoon garlic powder	Guacamole, salsa, black bean dip
Coriander-Lime	½ teaspoon freshly grated lime zest ½ teaspoon ground coriander ⅛ teaspoon freshly ground black pepper	Guacamole, mango salsa, black bean dip

CHAPTER 7

Gooey Goodness

Grilled Cheese on the Panini Press

Pimiento Cheese Panini

Pimiento cheese—a cheese spread made from sharp cheddar, diced pimientos, and mayonnaise—is real Southern comfort food. Don't knock it till you've tried it; that tangy flavor just might reel you in. It's most often served as a cold sandwich between two slices of white bread, but it also makes a pretty amazing—if a little oozy—grilled cheese.

¼ cup mayonnaise

2 tablespoons diced pimientos plus ¼ teaspoon of the juice from the jar

4 ounces (about 1 cup) shredded extra-sharp cheddar cheese

A pinch of cayenne pepper

4 tablespoons (½ stick) butter, at room temperature

8 slices rustic white bread, sliced from a dense bakery loaf

—
4 panini

Blend the mayonnaise, pimientos, pimiento juice, and cheddar in a food processor until it's generally orange in color and has a semi-chunky consistency.

Heat the panini press to medium-high heat.

FOR EACH SANDWICH: Spread butter on two slices of bread to flavor the outside of the sandwich. Flip over one slice and spread a layer of pimiento cheese on the other side. Close the sandwich with the other slice of bread, buttered side up.

Grill two panini at a time, with the lid closed, until the bread is toasted and the cheese melts and starts to ooze out, about 3 minutes.

Rajas Grilled Cheese Panini

The word rajas in Spanish translates as "strips," as in strips of roasted chiles and onions that bring a punch of south-of-the-border flavor to all kinds of dishes. Grilling rajas is an easy job on the panini press—it takes just minutes to get them nicely charred. Pile them on a sandwich with pepper Jack for a spicy grilled cheese or, to tone down the heat, opt for Monterey Jack.

4 tablespoons (½ stick) butter, at room temperature

8 slices sourdough bread, sliced from a dense bakery loaf

8 ounces pepper Jack cheese, sliced

1 recipe *Rajas* (page 75)

—

4 panini

FOR EACH SANDWICH: Spread butter on two slices of bread to flavor the outside of the sandwich. Flip over one slice and top the other side with cheese, a generous pile of *rajas*, and more cheese. Close the sandwich with the other slice of bread, buttered side up.

Grill two panini at a time, with the lid closed, until the cheese is melted and the bread is toasted, 4 to 5 minutes.

Honey Walnut–Crusted Aged Cheddar Panini

A visit to Beecher's Handmade Cheese, a small but renowned shop at Pike Place Market in Seattle, gave me a newfound appreciation for grilled cheese. Their basic grilled cheese sandwich—composed simply of their super-sharp, tangy Flagship cheese panini-grilled between two slices of rustic bread—compelled me to slow things down in my otherwise hectic day and savor every last gooey bite.

The day after I returned home I picked up a block of their cheese from my local grocery store so I could relive the experience on my own grill. I added a honey-walnut crust on the bread to lift the cheese onto a lightly sweet and crunchy pedestal. Any good-quality aged cheddar will work well in this recipe, but if you have the chance to try it with Beecher's, do!

¼ cup finely chopped walnuts

4 tablespoons (½ stick) butter, at room temperature

1 tablespoon honey

8 slices rustic white bread, sliced from a dense bakery loaf

8 ounces aged sharp cheddar cheese, thinly sliced

—

4 panini

Heat the panini press to medium-high heat.

In a small bowl, mix the chopped walnuts, butter, and honey until well combined.

FOR EACH SANDWICH: Spread a layer of honey-walnut butter on two slices of bread. Flip over one slice of bread and top the other side with cheese. Close the sandwich with the other slice of bread, buttered side up.

Grill two panini at a time, with the lid closed, until the cheese is melted and the bread is toasted, 4 to 5 minutes.

Jalapeño Popper Grilled Cheese Panini

It's not that spicy! I just wanted to put that out there from the get-go. I know when you see the word "jalapeño" you think this is going to be super-hot. If I were to use raw peppers, oh yes, there would be a fire in your mouth. But instead, I take the seeds out (where much of the heat comes from) and roast the peppers for a few minutes. Instead of an inferno, you get a milder, gently sweet heat.

What I also love about my panini version of the classic cheese-stuffed jalapeño popper appetizer is its tortilla chip crust spiced with cumin and cayenne. My friend Laura Werlin, a James Beard award-winning cheese expert, first introduced me to the brilliant idea of crusting a grilled cheese sandwich in tortilla chips (her Chips and Guacamole Grilled Cheese is out of this world). Here, that crunchy corn crust gives way to a lava of sweet roasted jalapeños and tangy melted cheese.

4 jalapeño peppers, halved lengthwise and seeded

2 ounces cream cheese, at room temperature

6 ounces (about 1½ cups) shredded sharp cheddar cheese

2 ounces corn tortilla chips (about 8 large chips)

4 tablespoons (½ stick) butter, at room temperature

¼ teaspoon ground cumin

A pinch of cayenne pepper

8 slices sourdough bread, sliced from a dense bakery loaf

—

4 panini

Set a rack on the top shelf of the oven or toaster oven and heat it to broil.

Place the jalapeños, cut sides down, on a baking sheet and broil until the skins are charred, 7 to 8 minutes. Transfer the jalapeños to a paper bag, close the bag, and let them steam until the skin of the peppers puckers and is easily removed, about 5 minutes.

Heat the panini press to medium-high heat.

Remove and discard the skins from the jalapeños, chop the peppers, and transfer them to a medium-size bowl. Add the cream cheese and sharp cheddar and mix them well.

Seal the tortilla chips in a zipper-top plastic bag and roll a rolling pin back and forth over the bag until the chips are crushed into fine crumbs. In a small bowl, mix the tortilla chip crumbs, butter, cumin, and cayenne until they're well combined.

FOR EACH SANDWICH: Spread a layer of tortilla chip butter on two slices of bread to flavor the outside of the sandwich. Flip over one slice and spread on a generous layer of cheese mixture. Close the sandwich with the other slice of bread, buttered side up.

Grill two panini at a time, with the lid closed, until the cheese is melted and the outside is toasted and crispy, about 5 minutes.

Gruyère and Red Onion Confit Panini

You know you've found a kindred spirit when you discover you both share the same taste in grilled cheese sandwiches. I was interviewing Gina Freize, owner of Venissimo Cheese, my favorite cheese shop here in San Diego, when she began to describe the staff's favorite panini: sweet, silky, ribbons of red onion confit layered on ciabatta with one of the best-melting cheeses out there, Gruyère. It sounded remarkably similar to my own prevailing favorite—Gruyère with Caramelized Onions (see PaniniHappy.com for this recipe)—except that the onions were more jam-like, sweetened further with sugar and simmered in red wine and thyme. In that moment, I couldn't think of anything else I wanted to eat.

Gina described Gruyère and Red Onion Confit Panini as "French onion soup on a bun," to which I would add "with a glass of wine."

1 ciabatta loaf, cut into 4 portions, or 4 ciabatta rolls

8 ounces Gruyère cheese, thinly sliced

1 cup Red Onion Confit (recipe follows)

—

4 panini

Heat the panini press to medium-high heat.

FOR EACH SANDWICH: Split a ciabatta portion to create top and bottom halves. Arrange enough cheese slices inside the bottom half to cover the surface. Top the cheese with a few tablespoons of red onion confit and more cheese. Close the sandwich with the top half of the ciabatta.

Grill two panini at a time, with the lid closed, until the cheese is melted and the ciabatta is toasted, 5 to 7 minutes.

Red Onion Confit

It's worth the time it takes to make this red onion confit, and you won't mind at all about having some left over. You'll want to add these onions to everything—other panini, meats or poultry, pizzas, and pastas.

2 tablespoons butter

1 tablespoon extra-virgin olive oil

3 medium-size red onions, halved and thinly sliced

½ cup dry red wine, such as Cabernet Sauvignon or Malbec

2 tablespoons chopped fresh thyme

2 tablespoons sugar

3 tablespoons balsamic vinegar

Coarse salt and freshly ground black pepper

—
About 2 cups

Heat the butter and olive oil in a large skillet or Dutch oven over medium heat until the butter is melted. Add the onions and cook, stirring often, until they're softened, 8 to 10 minutes.

Add the wine, thyme, and sugar and continue cooking, stirring occasionally, until the onions are very soft and tender, about 30 minutes more. Lower the heat, if necessary, to avoid scorching.

Pour in the balsamic vinegar and season the onions with salt and pepper to taste. Continue cooking and stirring for another 5 minutes to allow the liquid to absorb. The onions will be silky, glistening, and deep reddish-purple.

Use the onions right away or store them in the refrigerator, covered, for up to 5 days.

Green Goddess Grilled Cheese Panini

Bursting with bright, fresh green herbs and kicked up with the bold flavors of garlic and anchovies, Green Goddess salad dressing has been making a bit of a comeback in recent years. It was first created at the Palace Hotel in San Francisco back in the 1920s. Now it's again popping up at restaurants and being bottled commercially by major brands. As I toyed with ideas for making green panini for St. Patrick's Day one year, it struck me to invent grilled cheese panini based on this very green classic.

1 garlic clove, finely chopped

1 anchovy fillet, finely chopped

Zest of 1 lime (about 1 teaspoon)

3 tablespoons chopped fresh flat-leaf parsley

2 tablespoons chopped fresh tarragon

2 tablespoons chopped fresh cilantro

1 tablespoon chopped fresh basil

1 tablespoon finely chopped shallot

¼ teaspoon Dijon mustard

2 ounces cream cheese, cut into small cubes

4 ounces (about 1 cup) shredded mozzarella cheese

4 ounces (about 1 cup) shredded sharp white cheddar cheese

4 to 6 tablespoons butter, at room temperature

8 to 12 slices sourdough bread, sliced from a dense bakery loaf

—

4 to 6 panini

Place the garlic and anchovies in a mini food processor and pulse a few times until they're very finely minced, almost a paste (if you don't have a food processor, just mince the ingredients as finely as possible with a knife).

Add the lime zest, parsley, tarragon, cilantro, basil, shallot, mustard, and cream cheese and pulse again until well blended. Transfer the mixture to a medium-size bowl and stir in the mozzarella and cheddar cheeses.

Heat the panini press to medium-high heat.

FOR EACH SANDWICH: Spread butter on two slices of bread to flavor the outside of the sandwich. Flip over one slice and spread a generous amount of the cheese mixture on the other side. Close the sandwich with the other slice of bread, buttered side up.

Grill two panini at a time, with the lid closed, until the cheese is melted and oozy and the bread is toasted, 5 to 6 minutes.

NOTE:

The total number of panini will depend on the size of your bread. Take care not to overfill each sandwich.

CHAPTER 8

A Little Something Sweet

Dessert on the Panini Press

Caramel Apple-Stuffed French Toast

I was leafing through the pages of my favorite specialty cookware catalog when my eyes stopped on a photo of the most gorgeous, thick-cut, caramelized banana–stuffed French toast, created by chef Bryan Voltaggio. Better yet, it was grilled on a panini press! I, of course, had no choice but to try it out and I, of course, loved it.

Here, I've adapted Chef Voltaggio's recipe to feature caramelized cinnamon apples stuffed within the fluffy challah French toast. Once you drizzle the praline-like toasted pecan maple syrup down those lightly crisp grilled ridges—we're talking dessert for breakfast. Tell your family to have a little patience while you prepare this special-occasion French toast. It will be well worth the wait. (For a simpler, everyday version, see my Grilled French Toast, page 127.)

CARAMELIZED APPLES

3 tablespoons butter

2 tablespoons sugar

1 teaspoon ground cinnamon

A pinch of coarse salt

2 medium-size apples (about 1 pound), peeled, cored, and sliced (I like to use Gala)

⅓ cup heavy cream

FRENCH TOAST

4 slices day-old challah, each about 1½ inches thick

4 large eggs

1⅓ cups milk

¼ cup sugar

½ teaspoon ground cinnamon

¼ teaspoon pure vanilla extract

1 recipe Toasted Pecan Maple Syrup (recipe follows)

—

4 servings

CARAMELIZED APPLES: Melt the butter in a large skillet over medium heat. Stir in the sugar, cinnamon, salt, and apples. Cook, stirring frequently, until the apples are brown and tender and a deep brown caramel forms, 7 to 10 minutes. Add the cream and simmer until the sauce thickens slightly, about 2 minutes. Transfer the apples to a medium-size bowl and let them cool.

FRENCH TOAST: Using a small, sharp knife, create a pocket in each bread slice by cutting a 2-inch-long slit in the crust on one side of the bread and continuing to cut three-quarters of the way through the bread. Stuff the pockets with a few of the apple slices (this is a messy business!). Reserve the rest of the apples for serving.

Heat the panini press to medium-high heat.

In a large shallow bowl, whisk together the eggs, milk, sugar, cinnamon, and vanilla. Soak two of the bread slices for about 2 minutes per side.

Place the eggy bread on the panini press and, if possible, adjust the top plate so that it lightly presses the bread. Grill the toast until it's browned and cooked through, about 5 minutes. Transfer the toast to a plate and tent it with foil to keep it warm while you soak and grill the remaining two bread slices. Serve the French toast with more caramelized apples and the pecan maple syrup.

Toasted Pecan Maple Syrup

A special French toast deserves a special syrup to go along with it. It takes less than 10 minutes to give ordinary maple syrup a nutty boost with butter-toasted pecans.

1 tablespoon unsalted butter

½ cup chopped pecans

A pinch of coarse salt

¾ cup pure maple syrup

—

About 1 cup

Melt the butter in a small skillet or saucepan over medium heat and cook until it's lightly browned, a few minutes. Add the pecans and cook, stirring occasionally, until the pecans are lightly toasted and aromatic, about 3 minutes. Stir in the salt and maple syrup. Turn up the heat to medium-high and cook the syrup until it's slightly thickened, about 2 minutes. Transfer the syrup to a bowl and keep it warm while you prepare the French toast. If you've made the syrup in advance, reheat it on the stove or in the microwave.

Grilled Apple Turnovers

This is an updated version of the very first non-panini recipe I ever posted on PaniniHappy.com. I guess I figured out early on that there was more to this panini press machine than just sandwiches. Lots of familiar foods could be prepared just as well—perhaps even faster and better—on a panini press.

Oven-baked apple turnovers are always a treat. But if you grill them, the resulting ridges give you the excuse to fill those valleys with vanilla ice cream.

3 medium-size apples (about 1½ pounds), a combination of sweet and tart, such as Gala and Granny Smith, peeled, cored, and thinly sliced

3 tablespoons freshly squeezed lemon juice

2 tablespoons sugar

1 tablespoon all-purpose flour

½ teaspoon ground cinnamon

⅛ teaspoon ground nutmeg

A pinch of coarse salt

A pinch of ground cardamom (optional)

1 (17.3-ounce) package frozen puff pastry sheets, thawed

1 large egg

1 tablespoon water

Ice cream, for serving

—

8 turnovers

MAKE IT AHEAD:

If you'd like to grill just a few turnovers at a time, you can wrap any assembled, uncooked turnovers tightly in plastic wrap and store them in the refrigerator for 2 to 3 days until you're ready to grill them.

In a medium-size bowl, toss the apple slices with the lemon juice. Add the sugar, flour, cinnamon, nutmeg, salt, and cardamom (if you're using it) and toss to coat the apples.

Heat the panini press to medium-high heat (if your grill has a temperature setting, set it to 400°F).

On a lightly floured surface, roll out each puff pastry sheet into a 12-inch square. Divide each square into four 6-inch squares.

Spoon 6 or 7 apple slices onto the center of each pastry square.

In a small bowl, whisk the egg and water together to make an egg wash. One pastry square at a time, brush a little egg wash along the edges of the square and fold it over diagonally to form a triangle. Press the edges together with your fingers and then crimp them with a fork to seal them.

Carefully place two turnovers on the grill. Lower the lid until it's very lightly touching them (if your press allows you to fix the height so that the upper plate hovers about ¼ inch above the turnovers, that's even better). As the turnovers bake they'll puff up and make contact with the upper plate—you want to give them a little room to expand. Grill until the pastry is puffed, golden, and crisp on the outside, about 12 minutes. Repeat this step for the remaining 6 turnovers.

Serve the turnovers hot with a scoop of ice cream on top, running down into those crinkly pastry ridges.

Grilled French Toast

The number one reason to cook French toast on a panini press instead of in a skillet: no need to flip! And the second-best reason is the lightly crisp, ridged surface created by the grill grates—it's perfect for holding maple syrup.

French toast works best on a panini press that allows you to adjust the height of the upper plate. It's one of those instances where a lighter-than-usual amount of pressure is required, to avoid squeezing the egg mixture out of the soft bread.

This is a wonderfully simple recipe for fluffy French toast made from day-old challah. For a slightly jazzed up, special-occasion version, try my Caramel Apple–Stuffed French Toast (page 124).

4 large eggs

1⅓ cups milk

¼ cup sugar

½ teaspoon ground cinnamon

¼ teaspoon pure vanilla extract

4 slices day-old challah, each about 1 inch thick

Pure maple syrup, for serving

—
4 servings

Heat the panini press to medium-high heat.

In a large, shallow bowl, whisk together the eggs, milk, sugar, cinnamon, and vanilla. Soak two of the bread slices for about 2 minutes per side.

Place the eggy bread on the panini press and, if possible, adjust the top plate so that it lightly presses the bread. Grill the toast, with the lid closed, until it's browned, about 5 minutes. Soak and grill the remaining bread slices. Serve with maple syrup.

Fluffernutter Panini

I get why the people of Massachusetts sought to have the Fluffernutter—a peanut butter and marshmallow crème sandwich concoction—designated as their official state sandwich. But in reality, these things ought to be illegal, they're so decadent. Well, far be it from me to judge . . . or deny that this sandwich sounded pretty appealing to me. So I went ahead and dressed up my grilled version with nuggets of crunchy candied peanuts dispersed throughout the sandwich and added a cinnamon-sugar crust. Go big, right?

4 tablespoons unsalted butter, at room temperature

2 tablespoons sugar

2 teaspoons ground cinnamon

A pinch of coarse salt

8 slices white bread, each about 1 inch thick

½ cup peanut butter

½ cup Marshmallow Fluff or other marshmallow crème

¼ cup Candied Peanuts (recipe follows)

—

4 panini

In a small bowl, mix the butter, sugar, cinnamon, and salt until they're well combined.

Heat the panini press to medium-high heat.

FOR EACH SANDWICH: Spread a layer of cinnamon-sugar butter on two slices of bread. Flip them over and spread a generous layer of peanut butter on one slice and a good amount of Marshmallow Fluff on the other. Scatter a small handful of candied peanuts over the peanut butter and close the sandwich with the other slice of bread, marshmallow side down.

Grill two panini at a time, with the lid closed, until the Marshmallow Fluff is melted and the bread is toasted, 2 to 3 minutes.

Candied Peanuts

If you find yourself with extra candied peanuts on hand, save them to top Grown-Up Grilled Banana Splits (page 130). Or keep them around for a sweet snack.

¼ cup sugar

¼ teaspoon coarse salt

1 tablespoon water

½ teaspoon pure vanilla extract

1 cup unsalted roasted peanuts

—

1 cup

Lay out a large sheet of aluminum foil and coat it with nonstick cooking spray. Set aside.

Combine all of the ingredients in a large, heavy-bottomed skillet over medium-high heat. Cook, stirring constantly, as the mixture goes from syrupy to dry and sandy and finally to a deep brown, smooth caramel stage, 10 to 12 minutes. Carefully pour the candied peanuts onto the prepared foil and allow them to cool for 5 minutes. Transfer the peanuts to an airtight container, breaking the candy apart if needed, and store them at room temperature for up to 2 weeks.

Grown-Up Grilled Banana Splits

Something pretty incredible happens when you grill a super-ripe banana in its peel. An already sweet treat turns near candy-like as the pulp softens, the juices are released, and it caramelizes inside the peel. Once you break it open, all you need is a spoon (and maybe a scoop of ice cream and some salted peanuts) to enjoy a very simple and—dare I say, grown-up—version of a banana split. If you're feeling very decadent, sub in my Candied Peanuts (see page 128) for the plain peanuts.

4 very ripe bananas (with lots of brown spots)

4 scoops vanilla ice cream

3 tablespoons chopped salted dry-roasted peanuts

—
4 servings

Heat the panini press to medium-high heat.

Set the bananas directly on the grill (in their peels) and close the lid. Grill the bananas until they feel rather soft when you give them a poke, about 8 minutes. You'll start to hear sizzling as the moisture from inside the bananas seeps through the peel.

Using tongs, take the bananas off the grill and transfer them to serving plates or bowls.

Slide a sharp knife down the center of each banana and peel back the banana peel to expose the soft, hot pulp, which should be swimming in its own caramel. Dollop on a scoop of vanilla ice cream and sprinkle the chopped salted peanuts over the top. Enjoy the whole hot-and-cold, sweet-and-salty dessert right out of the banana peel.

Mini Yellow Layer Cake with Chocolate Buttercream

None of my friends could quite picture what I was talking about when I told them I had baked a layer cake on the panini press. "How . . . what . . . *why?*"

It's incredibly easy to do. You just fill ramekins with cake batter and close the grill lid. In less than 20 minutes you've got rich, delicious yellow cake ready to be cooled and frosted in chocolate. I adapted the small-batch cake recipe from the uber-talented Jessica Merchant of the blog HowSweetEats.com for these personal mini cake layers.

Since this recipe involves baking, I suggest that you prepare it on a panini press that allows you to set a specific temperature.

YELLOW CAKE

¼ cup all-purpose flour

A heaping ¼ teaspoon baking powder

A pinch of coarse salt

1 large egg

2 tablespoons sugar

2 tablespoons unsalted butter, melted

1 teaspoon pure vanilla extract

1½ tablespoons milk

CHOCOLATE BUTTERCREAM

3 tablespoons unsalted butter, melted

3 tablespoons unsweetened cocoa powder

1 cup sifted confectioners' sugar

1½ tablespoons milk

¼ teaspoon pure vanilla extract

Sprinkles (optional)

—

1 to 2 servings

YELLOW CAKE: Heat the panini press to 350°F. Make sure that the grill sits flat on your work surface, not tilted. Spray two 6-ounce ramekins (3½ inches in diameter) with nonstick cooking spray.

In a small bowl, whisk together the flour, baking powder, and salt.

In a medium-size bowl, whisk together the egg and sugar until they are combined. Stir in the melted butter and vanilla. Add the dry ingredients and stir until the batter is smooth. Stir in the milk.

Divide the batter equally between the two ramekins. Set the ramekins on the panini grill and close the lid so that the upper plate makes contact with the rims of the ramekins. Bake the cakes until they are set and spring back when touched in the center, 17 to 19 minutes. Remove the ramekins from the grill and allow them to cool for 5 minutes, then invert the cakes onto a wire rack to cool completely.

CHOCOLATE BUTTERCREAM: In a small bowl, whisk together the butter and cocoa. Add the confectioners' sugar, milk, and vanilla and whisk until the frosting is smooth.

Assemble the layers and frost the cake with chocolate buttercream. Sprinkles are optional, but they sure are fun.

Homemade Ice Cream Cones

This is worth screaming from the rooftops: You can make ice cream cones with your panini press! Easily! With no special ingredients! And they're really, really good! Get ready for your inner child to leap with joy once that familiar sweet cookie smell from the ice cream parlor wafts about your kitchen. If you've ever watched the ice cream folks make cones, all they do is place some batter on a shallow waffle iron, press out the batter and shape the cone. It finally occurred to me . . . couldn't we do the same thing on a panini press? Absolutely!

I've adapted an easy, flavorful ice cream cone recipe created by pastry chef Gale Gand so it can be prepared on the panini press, with the help of a DIY cone mold. See the Note at the end of the recipe for instructions on how to make your mold. This recipe requires a panini press that closes very tightly in order to make a wafer thin enough to turn into a cone.

1½ cups confectioners' sugar

1½ cups all-purpose flour

¼ teaspoon ground cinnamon

A pinch of ground nutmeg

1 tablespoon cornstarch

1 cup heavy cream

1½ teaspoons pure vanilla extract

—

14 ice cream cones

NOTE:

To make a mold for the cone, mark a circle approximately 4⅝ inches in diameter on a piece of cardstock-weight paper. Use scissors to cut out the circle, then form the paper into a cone shape by overlapping two sides and twisting the circle until you've formed a point on one end. Tape the cone closed so that it retains its shape.

In a medium-size bowl, whisk together the confectioners' sugar, flour, cinnamon, nutmeg, and cornstarch. Set aside.

In another medium-size bowl, with a whisk or electric mixer whip the cream and vanilla together until it is mousse-like. Add the dry ingredients to the cream and stir to make a batter. Let the batter sit at room temperature for 30 minutes.

Heat the panini press to medium-high heat.

FOR EACH ICE CREAM CONE: Place a heaping tablespoonful of batter onto the grill and close the lid, completely pressing the batter. Grill until the pressed cone is browned but still malleable, about 90 seconds; it will be an oblong shape. Carefully transfer the pressed cone to a cutting board or piece of waxed paper. Position your cone mold (see the Note below) in the center of the pressed cone, leaving about ½ inch space between the long edge of the pressed cone and the pointed end of the cone mold. Working quickly and carefully (the cone will be very hot!), roll the pressed cone around the cone mold to shape it. Leave the cone on the mold for about 10 seconds to set the shape.

Enjoy your favorite ice cream in your freshly made cones! The cones are best enjoyed the same day that they are made, but they'll still be fresh the next day if stored in an airtight container at room temperature.

Mini Carrot Layer Cake with Maple Cream Cheese Frosting

If you have just one carrot on hand in your crisper, the healthiest thing to do with it would be to peel and eat it raw. A somewhat more indulgent approach would be to make yourself a mini carrot layer cake on your panini press.

After I posted my first mini layer cake on PaniniHappy.com, a consumer packaged-goods company approached me about creating another one for a "new take on cupcakes" feature they were putting together. This is the cake I came up with—classic carrot cake, full of walnuts and spices, and topped with an autumn-sweet maple cream cheese frosting. Without the egg yolk, this is a bit lighter in texture than the Mini Yellow Layer Cake (page 131) but just as rich and moist.

Since this recipe involves baking, I suggest that you prepare it on a panini press that allows you to set a specific temperature.

CARROT CAKE

¼ cup all-purpose flour

A heaping ¼ teaspoon baking powder

A pinch of coarse salt

A pinch of ground cinnamon

A pinch of ground ginger

A pinch of ground nutmeg

1 large egg white

2 tablespoons packed light brown sugar

2 tablespoons canola oil

1½ teaspoons milk

¼ teaspoon pure vanilla extract

⅓ cup packed shredded carrots (from about 1 carrot)

1 tablespoon raisins

1 tablespoon chopped walnuts

MAPLE CREAM CHEESE FROSTING

1 tablespoon chopped walnuts

2 ounces cream cheese, at room temperature

1 tablespoon unsalted butter, at room temperature

⅓ cup sifted confectioners' sugar

2 teaspoons pure maple syrup

—

1 to 2 servings

CARROT CAKE: Heat the panini press to 350°F. Make sure that the grill sits flat on your work surface, not tilted. Spray two 6-ounce ramekins (3½ inches in diameter) with nonstick cooking spray.

In a small bowl, whisk together the flour, baking powder, salt, cinnamon, ginger and nutmeg.

In a medium-size bowl, whisk together the egg white, brown sugar, oil, milk, and vanilla until they are combined. Add the dry ingredients and stir until the batter is blended. Mix in the carrots, raisins, and walnuts.

Divide the batter equally between the two ramekins. Set the ramekins on the panini press and close the lid so that the upper plate makes contact with the rims of the ramekins. Bake the cakes until they are set and spring back when touched in the center, 17 to 19 minutes. Remove the ramekins from the grill and allow them to cool for 5 minutes, then invert the cakes onto a wire rack to cool completely.

MAPLE CREAM CHEESE FROSTING: Spread the chopped walnuts in a small skillet. Cook the walnuts over medium-low heat, shaking the pan frequently to move them around, until they are fragrant and toasted, 10 to 12 minutes. Set the toasted walnuts aside to cool.

(continued)

In a small bowl, beat together the cream cheese and butter with a hand mixer. Add the confectioners' sugar and maple syrup and beat until the frosting is smooth. Assemble the layers and frost the cake with the frosting.

Give the toasted walnuts an extra fine chop and sprinkle them on top of the cake.

Grilled Angel Food Cake with Lemon Curd

Something really cool happens when you grill angel food cake: the outside gets ever-so-gently crisped and practically dissolves on your tongue like cotton candy. It transforms an otherwise average, store-bought cake into something far more appealing—especially when you top it with some sweet-tart homemade lemon curd.

8 slices angel food cake, each about 1 inch thick (see Note)

1 cup Lemon Curd, purchased or homemade (recipe follows)

½ pint (about ¾ cup) fresh raspberries

—

4 servings

Heat the panini press to high heat.

In batches, place the angel food cake slices on the grill. Close the lid so that the upper plate is resting on the cake without pressing it. Grill the cake slices until they're toasted and grill marks appear, about 1 minute. Alternatively, leave the grill open and grill the cake slices for about 90 seconds per side.

Serve the grilled angel food cake with a few spoonfuls of lemon curd and some fresh raspberries.

NOTE

If you bake your own angel food cake from scratch, save the yolks to make the lemon curd.

Lemon Curd

Chocolate lovers have their Nutella. If you're a lemon lover, then homemade lemon curd needs to be part of your repertoire. The silky-smooth citrus spread is a terrific topper for treats like angel food cake and pound cake and also makes an easy layer cake filling. It takes a little effort to make your own homemade lemon curd but, as with so many things, it tastes way better than store-bought.

5 large egg yolks

¾ cup sugar

2 tablespoons finely grated lemon zest

⅓ cup freshly squeezed lemon juice

5 tablespoons butter, cubed and chilled

—
About 1½ cups

Fill a medium-size saucepan with an inch of water and bring it to a simmer over medium-high heat (or, if you have a double boiler, heat an inch of water in the lower saucepan).

Meanwhile, whisk together the egg yolks and sugar in a medium-size heatproof bowl (or the upper saucepan of your double boiler) until smooth. Whisk in the lemon zest and juice until the mixture is smooth.

Once the water is simmering, turn down the heat to low and place the bowl on top of the saucepan; the bowl should not touch the water (if you're using a double boiler, assemble the upper and lower saucepans). Whisk the egg mixture continually until it thickens, about 15 minutes. It should be thick enough to coat the back of a wooden spoon.

Remove the bowl or upper saucepan from the heat and stir in one cube of butter at a time, incorporating each cube before adding the next. If you're using a double boiler, transfer the curd to a bowl. If you're not serving the curd immediately, press a layer of plastic wrap on the surface of the curd to prevent a skin from forming and refrigerate until you're ready to use it.

The lemon curd will thicken quite a bit in the refrigerator. To restore it to a spoonable consistency, set your bowl of curd inside a larger bowl. Fill the larger bowl with enough hot water to rise about halfway up the sides of the bowl of curd. Give the curd a stir every few minutes, refreshing the larger bowl with new hot water, until the curd is soft enough to serve. It will stay fresh in the refrigerator for up to 2 weeks.

Measurement Equivalents

Liquid Conversions

U.S.	Metric
1 tsp	5 ml
1 tbs	15 ml
2 tbs	30 ml
3 tbs	45 ml
¼ cup	60 ml
⅓ cup	75 ml
⅓ cup + 1 tbs	90 ml
⅓ cup + 2 tbs	100 ml
½ cup	120 ml
⅔ cup	150 ml
¾ cup	180 ml
¾ cup + 2 tbs	200 ml
1 cup	240 ml
1 cup + 2 tbs	275 ml
1¼ cups	300 ml
1⅓ cups	325 ml
1½ cups	350 ml
1⅔ cups	375 ml
1¾ cups	400 ml
1¾ cups + 2 tbs	450 ml
2 cups (1 pint)	475 ml
2½ cups	600 ml
3 cups	720 ml
4 cups (1 quart)	945 ml
(1,000 ml is 1 liter)	

Weight Conversions

U.S./U.K.	Metric
½ oz	14 g
1 oz	28 g
1½ oz	43 g
2 oz	57 g
2½ oz	71 g
3 oz	85 g
3½ oz	100 g
4 oz	113 g
5 oz	142 g
6 oz	170 g
7 oz	200 g
8 oz	227 g
9 oz	255 g
10 oz	284 g
11 oz	312 g
12 oz	340 g
13 oz	368 g
14 oz	400 g
15 oz	425 g
1 lb	454 g

Oven Temperature Conversions

°F	Gas Mark	°C
250	½	120
275	1	140
300	2	150
325	3	165
350	4	180
375	5	190
400	6	200
425	7	220
450	8	230
475	9	240
500	10	260
550	Broil	290

NOTE: All conversions are approximate.

Index